Thomas Day Curtis

Hints on Diarying

Thomas Day Curtis

Hints on Diarying

ISBN/EAN: 9783337012373

Printed in Europe, USA, Canada, Australia, Japan

Cover: Foto ©ninafisch / pixelio.de

More available books at **www.hansebooks.com**

JERSEYS—One Ton 2,000, Marpetro 3,352, Boma 4,834. Property of Beech Grove Farm, Beech Grove, Ind.

HINTS
ON
DAIRYING.

BY T. D. CURTIS.

Complete success in dairying depends on right conditions.

SYRACUSE, N. Y.
PUBLISHED FROM THE OFFICE OF THE
FARMER AND DAIRYMAN.
1885.

PREFACE.

It was intended by the Author to publish an exhaustive practical work on Dairying. But his time was so occupied by other matters that he was compelled to abandon the idea. Much of the following pages was written while traveling, the intervals of waiting at hotels and railroad stations being devoted to this work. But on reperusing the chapters as they appeared in the columns of the FARMER AND DAIRYMAN, and making slight additions, he has concluded to give them to the Dairy Public in their present form, believing that they may be of some assistance to the tyro, and perhaps afford a hint, here and there, to the dairyman of more experience who wishes to keep abreast of his fellows in the march of progress. This little book is not intended to supersede any other work on the subject, but to play the part of an auxiliary and present in a condensed form the pith which the reader might not have time to get from a more elaborate volume. The favor with which his "Hints on Cheesmaking"—now out of date—was received, gives the author confidence that his later effort may serve to fill a place that now remains unoccupied. Providence seems to have selected him as one of the laborers in this field of education, and he conscientiously devotes a portion of his energies to the service with envy toward none, but entertaining the hope that his mite may not be unacceptable among so many larger contributions.

HINTS ON DAIRYING.

HISTORICAL.

DAIRYING runs back to a period in the development of the human race of which we have no record. Man early learned to not only slay animals and eat their flesh, but to appropriate to himself the food belonging to their young—a trait of selfishness which he has not yet overcome, and even manifests by preying in various ways upon his fellows. We have in the world large classes who add nothing to its real wealth, but live and luxuriate on the fat of the earth by drawing the results of labor from the toilers through cunningly devised schemes of finance, business and government.

IN ASIA.

Away back in the dimness of antiquity, of which even tradition gives no hint, comparative philology shows us that a civilized race, now known as the Aryan race, dwelt on the steppes of Central Asia, and that the ox and the cow constituted their chief means of subsistence. They lived in simple peace and innocence, their language having no terms of war and strife. But there came a time when separation began and migration followed. They were scattered to the four corners of the Eastern Continent, and their descendants now constitute the progressive nations of the earth. The parent nation appears to have utterly perished in giving birth to the nations of the future. No trace of it is left, save the remnants of its language inherited by its children; but they furnish indisputable evidence of a common parentage.

AMONG THE JEWS.

Our earliest authentic records about the dairy are of the use of milk and its products among the Jews. We are told, in the 8th verse of the 18th chapter of Genesis, that when Abraham entertained the three strangers, "he took butter and milk, and the calf which he had dressed, and set it before them." Moses, in his song, as recorded in the 23d chapter of Deuteronomy, 14th verse, says of Jacob that the Lord, among other things, gave him to eat "butter of kine and milk of sheep." Deborah, who declares in her song that "the stars in their courses did fight against Sisera," who was entertained and slain by Jael, says of the murderess (Judges, 25th verse and 8th chapter) "he asked water and she gave him milk, she brought forth butter in a lordly dish." In the 17th chapter and 5th verse of 2d Samuel, the writer tells us that David and his people, after the battle in the wood of Ephraim, were given "honey and butter, and sheep and cheese of kine," to eat. Zophar, in the 20th chapter of Job, 17th verse, declares of the wicked hypocrite, who "hath swallowed down riches," that his triumph is short, and "he shall not see the rivers, the floods, the brooks of honey and butter"—which, we infer, are designed for the righteous; and Job (29th chapter and 6th verse) bemoans the loss of his former prosperity, "when I washed my steps with butter." In the 55th Psalm, 24th verse, David says of his enemy that "the words of his mouth were smoother than butter." Solomon appears to have understood the whole business. In Proverbs, 30th chapter and 33d verse, he exclaims: "Surely, the churning of milk bringeth forth butter." Isaiah, in the 7th chapter and 15th verse, declares of the coming Immanuel, that "butter and honey shall he eat;" and again (22d verse) that "for the abundance of milk that they shall give he shall eat butter."

IN SOUTHERN EUROPE.

Chambers says: " In ancient times, the Hebrews seem to have made copious use of butter as food; but the Greeks and the Romans used it only as an ointment in their baths, and it is probable that the Greeks obtained their knowledge of the subject from the Scythians, Thracians, and Phrygians, whilst the Romans obtained it of Germany." This would indicate that the Germans at that time were engaged in dairying. But, even now, in Southern Europe, butter is sparingly used, and in Italy, Spain, Portugal and Southern France, it is sold by apothecaries as an ointment. Dairying is now extensively carried on in all the countries of Northern Europe.

IN AMERICA.

When the early settlers of America crossed the Atlantic, they brought with them their favorite domestic animals, including the family cow. But dairying for a long time, in this country, appears to have been confined mainly to producing supplies for the family of the dairyman. It was not until quite a recent date that dairying sprang into commercial importance. But, to-day, dairying cannot be considered second to any other industry as to either magnitude or importance; and it is a patent fact that, in those sections where dairying is most extensively and successfully carried on, the farming population is the most prosperous and happy.

Within the last twenty years, since associated dairying has been introduced, great progress has been made in the dairy—but not greater than in many other occupations, nor out of proportion with the growth of population. The growth of the dairy will probably never exceed the growth of population so long as the present heavy tide of immigration continues to set toward our shores.

FIGURES FROM THE CENSUS.

Let us refer to the census of 1880, and note the development of the dairy during the previous 30 years:

By the census of 1850, we had 6,385,094 cows, and produced 314,345,306 pounds of butter, and 105,535,893 pounds of cheese—a total of 418,881,199 pounds of product.

By the census of 1860, we had 8,585,735 cows, and produced 459,681,372 pounds of butter, and 103,663,927 pounds of cheese—a total of 563,345,299 pounds of product.

HISTORICAL.

By the census of 1870, we had 8,935,332 cows and produced 514,692,683 pounds of butter, and 162,927,382 pounds of cheese—a total of 677,620,065 pounds of product—and this notwithstanding the **war** of the rebellion came in this decade.

By the census of 1880, we had 12,443,120 cows, **and** produced 806,662,071 pounds of butter, and 243,157,850 **pounds of cheese**—a total of 1,049,819,921 pounds of product.

GROWTH IN THIRTY YEARS.

This **is an** increase in annual product of 630,948,622 pounds in thirty years, or 212,057,523 pounds more than double the amount, in 1880, that was manufactured in 1850. History records no **parallel to** this anywhere **on** the face of the globe.

Let us put some of **these figures** into tabular form. We had in

	Cows		Inhabitants
1880	12,443,120	to	50,155,783
1850	6,385,094	to	23,191,876
Increase in 30 years	6,058,026		26,963,907

We did not quite double the number of cows, but considerably more than doubled the population. The number of inhabitants was, in

| 1850 | 3.63 per cow |
| 1880 | 4.03   " |

The increase in 30 years is .40 inhabitant to each cow. **That is to** say, the population, as compared with the number of cows, was .40 larger in 1880 than it was in 1850.

PRODUCT PER COW AND PER CAPITA.

And now let us compare the product per cow and per capita. It was in

	Lbs. per cow	Lbs. per capita
1850........418,881,199 lbs., or	65.77	or 18.06
1880.......1,049,829,921 lbs., or	84.37	or 20.93
Increase in 30 years............	18.60	2.87

HOME CONSUMPTION VS. EXPORTS.

But it should be borne in mind that in 1850 very nearly all our dairy products were consumed at home; whereas in 1880, we exported a large amount. As the exports do not all come in the year of production, we will take the average amount of exports for 1879 and 1880:

	Lbs. Butter.	Lbs. Cheese.
Exports, 1879........	38,248,016	141,654,474
" 1880........	39,236,658	127,553,907
Divided by........	2)77,484,674	269,208,381
Yearly average......	38,742,337	134,604,190
Add butter and cheese together..	38,742,337	

We have a yearly av. export of..173,346,527 pounds of product. If we take this from the total product of 1880......................1,049,829,921 pounds
                                                        173,346,527 pounds

we have............................. 876,483,394 pounds of product for home consumption, or more than five times as much as we export. This is a consumption of 17.47

pounds per capita for our 50,155,783 inhabitants, or .59 of a pound less than in 1850, when it was 18.60 pounds per capita. Does not this indicate the folly of catering for a foreign market to the neglect of our own?

FORMS OF MILK CONSUMPTION.

It is estimated by good judges that 45 per cent. of our milk product is consumed in its natural state, 50 per cent. is used in butter making, and 5 per cent. is made into cheese. The fact of there being a foreign demand for so large a proportion of our cheese, has led everybody astray, and magnified the cheese factory into the position of supreme importance.

THE PRIVATE DAIRY VS. THE FACTORY.

Let us again turn to the census of 1880, and see how the factory product compares in amount and importance with the product of the private dairy. It appears by the census of 1880 that the number of pounds of dairy products made in factories was as follows:

Cheese made in factories ...215,885,361 lbs.
Butter   "   "   .... 29,411,784 "

Total factory product...245,307,145 lbs.

Cheese made on farms........27,272,489 lbs.
Butter   "   "   "   ....777,250,287 "

Total farm product......804,522,776 lbs.
Deduct factory product......245,307,145 "

Excess of private dairy..559,215,631 lbs.

or considerably more than double the total factory product.

Now, let us make a comparison by values, calling the cheese 10 cents and the butter 25 cents a pound. We made in factories:

    Cheese, 215,885,361 lbs., @ 10c. $21,588,536
    Butter,   29,411,784 lbs., @ 25c.   7,352,946

          Value of factory product....$29,941,482

There was made in the private dairies:

    Cheese, 27,272,489 lbs., @ 10c. $ 2,727,249
    Butter, 777,250,287 lbs., @ 25c. 194,312,571

Value of private dairy products $197,039,820
Deduct value of factory products   29,941,482

    In favor of private dairy.......$167,098,338

In short, the product of the private dairy is between three and four times larger than that of the factory, and nearly seven times its value. Important as the factory is and is likely to become, let us not forget the private dairy nor overlook the home interest in striving for a little foreign patronage.

Notwithstanding the fault with the census that is found by some, the census is the most reliable source of statistical information about the dairy that we have.

CONDITIONS.

IT is not every novice that can take up the business of dairying and carry it on successfully; yet, some of our most successful dairymen are comparative novices in the business. Quick observation and sound judgment are important qualities in a dairyman. These qualities are not always acquired by long experience, but are oftener the generous gifts of nature. Hence, it frequently happens that men of quick discernment step into a new business and achieve success where others have met only years of failure. Improvements in all callings are apt to be made by sharp lookers-on, who are not bred in the habits of routinism, nor prejudiced against radical innovations. They see at a glance where the plodder fails, and fearlessly apply the remedy—often a short-cut to ends that have hitherto been reached with much difficulty and hard labor. And here is where the real inventor finds his greatest field of usefulness.

PASTURES.

Sweet pastures, with a variety of nutritious grasses growing in them, are essentials to success in dairying—especially in butter making—in summer. Bitter and other mal-flavored weeds must be avoided, as they flavor both the milk and the product manufactured from it. The cows must not be worried, nor over-worked in rambling over poor pastures to get sufficient food.

WATER.

Plenty of clean water must be conveniently at hand for the cows to drink. The water must be sweet and clean enough for the human stomach. Abundance of such water is more essential in the pasture—for the cows to drink while secreting milk that contains 87 per cent. of water—than it is in the dairy-house, where a small amount of water will answer, if ice is used, and hence can more easily be obtained pure.

WINTER FOOD.

In winter, the food must be in proper condition, properly balanced between the nitrogenous and carbonaceous materials, and in full supply—all the cow can digest and assimilate. At least one ration a day should include sweet ensilage, roots, or other succulent food, to aid in the separation of the butter from the cream by action of the churn, it having been shown that all dry feed not only reduces the flow of milk, but makes churning slow and difficult, leaving a large percentage of fat in the buttermilk.

THE STABLE.

While in stable, the cow must also have plenty of pure air and sweet water, and not be chilled in obtaining either. Without pure air, the cow becomes debilitated and diseased, and the milk impure and unwholesome.

CONDITIONS.   15

Impure water both taints and corrupts the product. A proper temperature—certainly above freezing—should be kept up. Remember, the cow standing still cannot resist cold as she could if she were free to move about. It is cheaper to build warm stables—always providing for perfect ventilation, the air coming in at the head and passing off in the rear of the cow—and even to resort to artificial heating, than to compel the cow to burn an extra amount of carbonaceous food in her system to keep up the temperature of her body. Not only is fuel cheaper than food, but the system of the cow cannot devote to milk secretion the energy which is expending in secreting and consuming fat to maintain a proper amount of vital heat.

SHELTER.

Proper shelter in summer, from the scorching rays of the mid-day sun, and from beating storms and winds, is necessary. This should be easily accessible. Especially in early spring and late fall do the animals suffer severely from exposure to the cold winds and storms of all hours in the twenty-four.

DAIRY HOUSE.

Every dairyman should have a good dairy house distinct from the dwelling apartments. It need not, necessarily, be a separate building. but it should not be subject to the inflowing of odors from the kitchen and sitting rooms. The dairy house should be so constructed that the temperature may at all times be kept under perfect control. There should be no surrounding cesspools

or other mal-odorous sources of taint, and the ventilation **should** be free without perceptible drafts or currents of air. No matter what method of setting milk and churning may be adopted, there is a decided advantage in **having** the dairy house, or any other workshop, separate from the **dw**elling apartments, so that the work of the one shall in no way interfere with the work of the other. Almost all dairymen fail, to some extent, in not having the dairy house entirely separate. It would cost but little extra; and until dairymen look upon the business as their life work and build and plan accordingly, we need not expect the best possible success in dairying.

CLEANLINESS.

Cleanliness everywhere and at **all times is an** absolute necessity. There is not the least danger of **being too** clean. The writer has never yet seen a dairy **without** defects in this particular. Yet, most people **mean to be** clean, and suppose they are. Lack of information **is** often the cause of uncleanliness, and habit goes a great way in making people indifferent to untidy surroundings. It is safe to copy the neat points found in every dairy, as well as to avoid the offensive ones. As Gov. Seymour once said, "cleanliness is a comparative term." It is well to keep making comparisons on this point, until **no** unfavorable comparisons with anybody's dai**ry can be** found; and these comparisons should **extend** to the surroundings of the cows, the manner of milking, the handling of the milk, the cleansing of milk utensils, and all the processes of manipulation from beginning to end. The dairy house should not only look clean, but be, as it were, fragrant with neatness and sweetness. And it is all-important that the clothing and person should be clean and neat to a fault. A sweet temper, even is no drawback.

THE HERD.

Of course, a thorough knowledge of the business must be had or be acquired. The proper selection or rearing of dairy stock is essential to success. The cow should not only be a good milker, but give milk suited to the line of dairying pursued. If cheese making is the object, there must be a large flow of milk rich in caseine. In butter making, a large flow of milk is not essential, but there must be a large percentage of fat in it. And the breeding must be such as to keep up the status of the herd. Some depend on purchasing cows, and exercise great care and judgment in so doing. In exceptional cases, a herd may be kept up in this way. But somebody must breed and rear good cows, or soon none can be had at any price. As a rule, it may be said to be the duty of every dairyman to breed from the best blood obtainable, and to rear the heifer calves from his best cows. Unless this condition is fulfilled, the dairy as a whole must run down. It is only by constant care and breeding from the best that the present status can be maintained, and possibly a little progress made. It should be the ambition of every dairyman to constantly improve the value of his herd, and to make progress in every department of his dairy, while improving the quality of his product.

DAIRY STOCK.

THERE is no more important subject connected with the dairy than that of the selection and rearing of stock. The herd is the fountain head. If there is failure here there is failure everywhere. Many a dairyman has remained poor all his days because he spent his time and energies on an unprofitable herd. This is the first thing to be looked after. The selection of a herd is a matter of both knowledge and judgment—knowledge of the characteristics of breeds and of the requisites of a good dairy cow, and judgment as to whether the individual cow in question possesses these characteristics and requisites. We will give some of the generally acknowledged characteristics of the different breeds, first indicating, as far as we can in words, some of the points of a good dairy cow.

POINTS OF A MILKER.

The dairy cow should be deep and broad through the flank—deeper and broader than through the shoulders—but must have a comparatively large chest, giving capacity of lungs and stomach, for she must have good digestive powers **and** inhale plenty of fresh air. Her hips should be broad, setting her thighs well apart, and her thighs should be rather thin. This gives space for a large udder, which is indispensable, for it is unreasonable to expect a large flow of milk from an udder of small capacity. The udder should be soft and fleshless when empty, and extend high up in the rear. It should also extend well forward, and from it should extend further forward large, protruding milk-veins. If they are double and are crooked and knotty, all the better. These veins carry off the blood after it has passed through the udder and performed its part in elaborating milk, and their size indicates the amount of blood employed, and by inference the amount of milk secreted. So the escutcheon, which should extend out on the thighs and run with even edges and unbroken surface up to or near the vulva, is supposed to be some indication of the extent of the arterial system that contributes blood for the elaboration of milk. The neck should be slender, taper and thin, the horns small and slender, the face dishing or flat, the eyes wide apart and mild and intelligent in expression, the muzzle broad when viewed from the front but thin when viewed from the side, and the lips thick and strong. A long, slender tail is indicative of good breeding. A yellow skin, or one which secretes an oily yellow scurf—especially seen in the ears, along the back and at the end of the tail—is considered a sign of milk rich in fat. The skin should be soft and pliable, the hair fine, and the coat glossy. We prefer rather light to very dark colors. Our observation is that a black cow never gives as rich milk as one in which the white predominates. In other colors we have not noted such a difference. Viewed from the front, the general shape of the cow should be a little wedging—thinner in front and thicker in the rear. Viewed from the side, **the cow** should taper from rear to front, with the upper and lower lines **generally straight, with** little or no slope from the **rump to the tail.**

DUTCH-FRIESIAN.

For general or **all** purposes, the Dutch-Friesian cow is not excelled. She may be equaled, but where is her superior? We use the name Dutch-Friesian because it expresses precisely what we mean—the black and white cattle of Friesian origin which have been bred pure in Friesland **or** North Holland, and not the **cattle called** "Holstein" **in** this country, which have **been** picked up promiscuously **in the** different provinces of Germany, because of their **peculiar** markings, but without reference to their breeding. **Some** of these may be pure bred, **but** they are liable to **disappoint the honest purchaser, who** buys them for and pays the price **of** pure bloods. The Dutch-Friesian cow **is** large, readily takes on flesh when not in milk, and therefore makes splendid beef. She is Hardy, docile and easily cared for. No other **breed** equals her in yield of milk. Her milk **is of average** richness, and she **gives** so much of it **that it makes her** valuable as a butter **cow.** Microscopists **say the fat globules in** her milk are very small. This makes it **somewhat** difficult to separate the fats **from** the milk for the purposes of butter making. Though the fat globules are quite uniform in size, **it** requires a long time to raise the

Dutch-Friesian Bull, MOOIE, 26 D. F. H. B.
Property of the Unadilla Valley Stock Breeders' Association, Whitestown, N. Y.

Dutch-Friesian Cow, JACOBA HARTOG, 2 D. F. H. B.
Property of the Unadilla Valley Stock Breeders' Association, Whitestown, N. Y.

cream by the ordinary methods, and the separation is not complete; but this makes the skim-milk all the more valuable for cheese making, feeding, or to market. With the centrifuge, there would be no difficulty in getting out all the cream. For market, or family use, or for cheese making, the milk of the Dutch-Friesian cow, because of the slowness with which the cream separates from the milk, is superior. It is rich in caseine, and therefore very valuable for cheese making. We could not recommend any other breed with greater confidence. Dutch-Friesian grades—the result of using pure-blooded Dutch-Friesian bulls on common or other stock—make very valuable dairy stock.

THE JERSEY.

Perhaps as widely separated from the Dutch-Friesian cow as any breed is the Jersey. She certainly is the smallest of all as the Dutch-Friesian is the largest—unless we except the Shorthorn and Hereford. The Jersey gives a small mess of milk, but it is very rich in fat, and the fat readily separates from the milk, leaving the skim-milk very blue and poor. It is not generally considered very rich in caseine, and it is therefore as poor and worthless as skim-milk well can be. But, considering size, the Jersey is conceded to yield more butter than any other breed. The cream globules are said to be very large and very uniform in size. Hence, they not only readily separate from the milk, but churn easily. The Jersey is out of the question as a beef animal, there is so little of her carcass; but we never heard complaint of the quality of the meat. But lack of beef qualities we do not consider a very serious objection in a dairy cow. We get our profit from her in the dairy. We cannot reasonably expect all good qualities in one animal or one breed. Nature is nowhere thus partial in her gifts. We find some good quality predominating in every one of the several breeds, and we must select accordingly to suit our line of dairying and our circumstances. The Jersey is a fawn-like, beautiful **animal**, with a mild eye and intelligent face, but usually has a quite angular frame, as a consequence of her excessive dairy qualities. She is rather tender, and cannot bear the exposure and harsh treatment that some of the breeds can. But no animal ought to receive such treatment. Kindness and comfortable quarters are due to all domestic **animals, and such care**, with proper feed, is the most **profitable to the owner**. The Jersey will not stand harsh usage; but **for the man of refined** taste and good judgment, **who** wants **a** nice thing **and** to turn out fancy **goods**, she is most decidedly the **cow**, and will not disappoint him. Solid colors and black muzzles are the fashion in Jerseys, but we are not aware that there is any practical merit in these. They have been bred down in size, to suit the taste of the English Lord, who wants them as pets on his lawns. This is rather against than in **favor** of **the Jersey** as a dairy cow, as it must of necessity **reduce her capa**city for converting food into milk and **cream**.

THE GUERNSEY

There are but few of these animals as yet in this country, but the few that have been imported and bred here have proved very satisfactory and promising. They are pale red or buff red and white. The colors are about in equal proportions, though the red may predominate. They are considerably larger than the Jersey and possess all the good qualities of the latter. Indeed, there is pretty good evidence that these breeds have the same origin, and that the Jersey is the Guernsey bred down in size and bred also for solid colors. The Guernsey is just as beautiful in face and form as the Jersey, and we think rather hardier and possesses more capacity. For all practical purposes, we should be inclined to give preference to the Guernsey, which has no rival in her line, except the Jersey. This breed can lay claim to some beef qualities, because of its size. It is destined to become a popular favorite in the butter dairy and as a family cow.

THE AYRSHIRE.

This breed is a great favorite with many. It is small—scarcely larger than the Guernsey—and is remarkably nimble and hardy, thriving on scant feed and in rough pastures where some of the other breeds would starve. The Ayrshires are red or red and white and give a large flow of milk, fairly rich in caseine and in butter. The breed has its phenomenal cows, both as milkers and as butter makers. The cream globules of the milk are quite irregular in size, and hence do not readily separate from the milk by ordinary methods of cream raising. But this fact makes the milk all the better for family use, for marketing and for the cheese factory, or for both butter and cheese from the same milk. The Ayrshire, like the Dutch-Friesian, may be called a good general purpose cow. The greatest objections to this breed have been its nervousness and its small teats; but both of these may be overcome by gentle treatment and careful breeding—indeed, have been overcome in many cases. For rough, hilly pastures, there is no better cow than the Ayrshire. But although she can stand some hard fare, she responds quickly to gentle and generous usage. Well-selected and well-bred Ayrshires make a splendid dairy herd.

THE SHORTHORN.

This has long been a popular breed, and there may be said to be a strong popular prejudice in its favor. Its undisputed, and perhaps unequaled, beef qualities have been its strongest recommend. It was, however, originally a milch breed, and some families of the breed are still hard to excel for the dairy. But it is quite difficult to select and maintain a milking strain, so long have the Shorthorns been bred for "beef and beauty," and so effectually have the milking qualities been bred out of them. In some of the beef families, the cows do not give milk enough to support their calves. Yet, many dairymen cling to this breed and keep unprofitable dairies because they can get a good price for the old carcass as beef when the cow is no longer tolerable in the dairy herd. This is short-sightedness, and holding beef for market too long and at too great a cost. The profit should be in the dairy products, where a dairy herd is

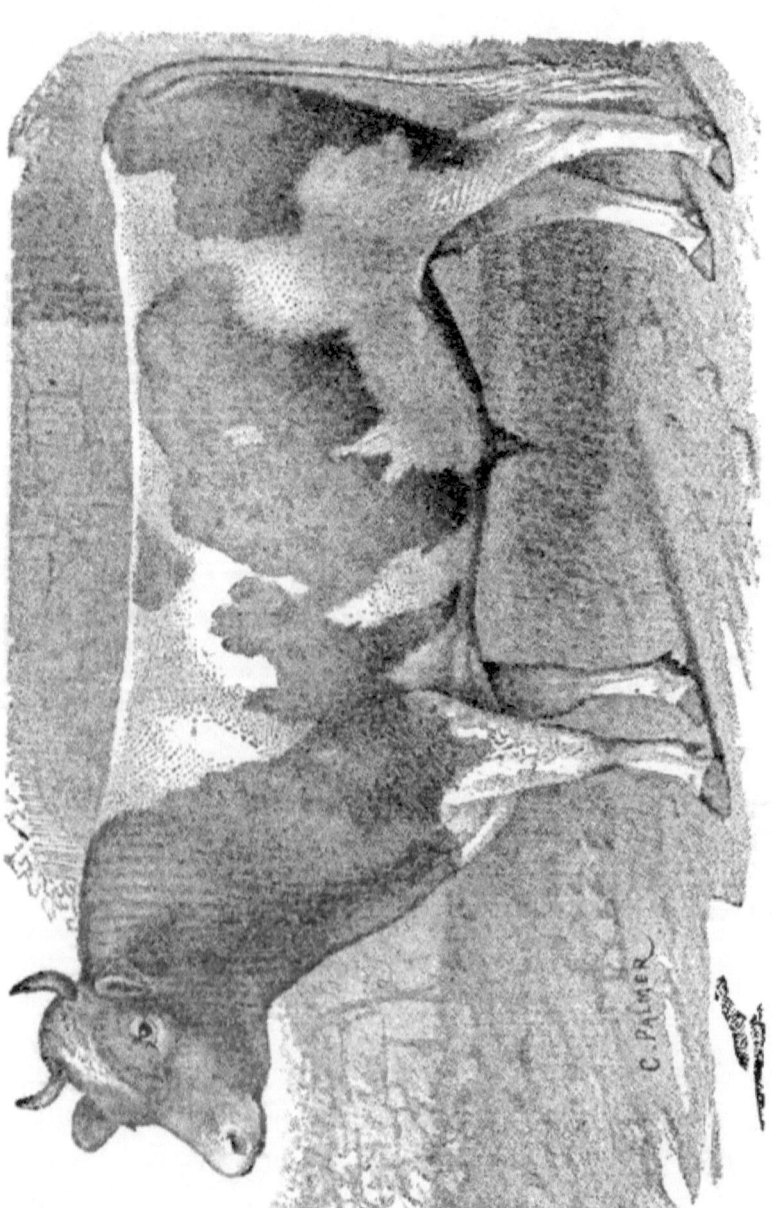

Guernsey Bull, "Lord Fernwood." Property of L. W. Ledyard, Fernwood Farm, Cazenovia, N. Y.

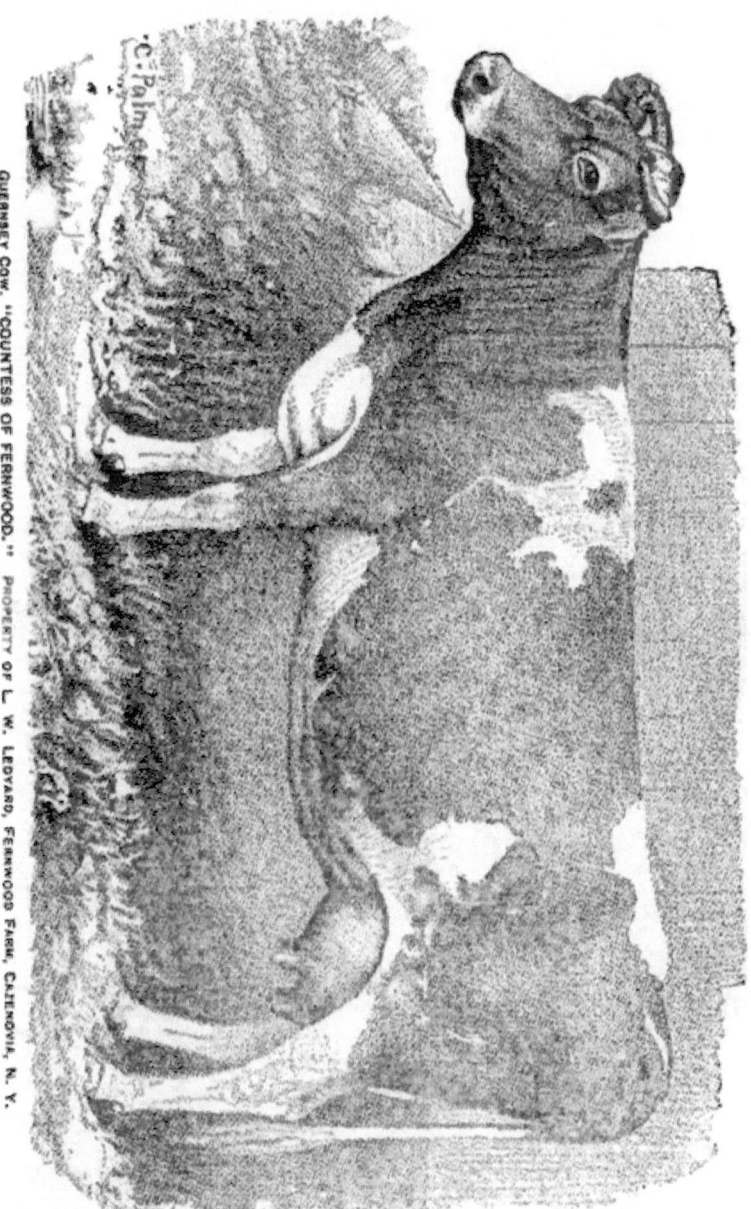

Guernsey Cow, "Countess of Fernwood." Property of L. W. Ledyard, Fernwood Farm, Cazenovia, N. Y.

kept, and beef should be altogether a **subordinate consideration**. The Shorthorn is usually **red or roan**, and occasionally red and white, though we always suspect other blood—Ayrshire, for instance—in the spotted animals. As a rule, we do **not** consider the Shorthorns as really profitable dairy cows, though there are many exceptions where a milking strain is cultivated. But there is no disputing their value for beef.

THE DEVON.

This is one of the choicest and **most reliable of the** dairy breeds. They are uniformly **red, of fair size, have** a sprightly appearance, and reproduce **their like** more certainly than any other **breed that we know.** As has been said, they are so prepotent, uniform, and distinct from the other breeds that they may be called a *race* of cattle. Their history runs back hundreds of years, until it is lost in tradition and uncertainty. But origin and history are of little consequence, since it **is** the living fact—**the** cattle themselves—that we have to deal with. The **cows give a** good sized mess of milk—large milkers have appeared **among** them as among other breeds—and their milk is very **rich.** It **is** not as **rich as** the Jersey's and the Guernsey's **milk, but** there **is more** of it, and it approximates **the** richness of the **milk** of these breeds more closely than that of any other. Hence, they are excellent butter cows, and justly favorites among those who are the most familiar with them and know how to breed them. Healthy, hardy, and easy to keep, they are adapted to almost any circumstances, and are excellent as butter or family cows, while the males, owing to their activity and endurance, make splendid oxen—both useful and fine looking. They make fine beef and a fair amount of it. They would be useful animals for crossing on the common stock and grades of the Northwest, where the climate is rigorous and both butter and beef are objects of importance. As workers, they would be very useful there. They will stand as much hardship as any breed we have, and as much as any breed ought to, but will do better under favorable than under unfavorable circumstances. Like all other breeds, they respond readily to kind and generous treatment, it being a universal law that want and abuse are sources of **loss** in the keeping of stock, the best results always following the best treatment. They will do well on level, hilly or rough pastures, because of their nimbleness and endurance; while the certainty of their breedidg makes it perhaps less difficult to perpetuate their good **qualities** than is the case with **any** of the other breeds. In short, they are the most prepotent and uniform of all, give a good-sized mess of very rich milk, are easy to keep, hardy and active, and fill a sphere which it would be difficult to fill without them. We do not know how their milk appears under the microscope, but we judge from **the** characteristics of these animals that the butter globules are above the average size and very uniform. Hence the cream rises readily, is easily churned, and makes a rich-colored, fine-flavored butter. It is a little remarkable that the breeders of these cattle have not succeeded in getting up a "boom;" but the probability is that no strenuous and persistent effort has been made in this direction. Their superior merits are unquestioned and unquestionable.

THE AMERICAN HOLDERNESS.

This is a new breed, and its reputation is mainly of a local character. But it is not without its representatives in most of the Northern and Northwestern States, and its fame has traveled quite extensively, considering the quiet and unpretentious manner in which it was originated and has been bred. In some particulars it is the most uniform of the breeds, even more uniform than the Devon. Especially is this true of the quality of the milk, which is as uniform throughout the herd as if it were drawn from a single cow, the quality varying, where the keep is the same, only with the age of the cow, and the lapse of time since calving. The yield of milk, though not excessive, is large and very rich—almost equal to that of the Jersey and Guernsey, and quite equal to that of the Devon. It churns easily, and the butter completely separates from the buttermilk, rendering a second churning of no avail. Three hundred pounds per cow a year of high-colored and fine-flavored butter is a fair average for a herd. Few, even of selected herds, of other animals equal this. We are not aware of phenomenal milkers among the Holderness cattle, unless all can be called such, their chief characteristic being uniformity. They breed, it may be said, perfectly true to type, so that all are excellent. The reason for this uniformity is plain, and is found in the origin of the breed in the closest possible inbreeding for thirty years. **They** originated **from** a cow with calf which was bought by Mr. Truman A. Cole, of Solsville, N. Y., of a drover who had just purchased it at auction in Knoxboro, N. Y., where a herd of pure-bloods, because of the death of the owner, had been sold under the auctioneer's hammer. The cow dropped a bull calf, which was bred to its mother, then to both mother and sister; and this system of close inbreeding, **even** sire to daughter, as well as brother to sister, has been continued down to the present time, or for thirty years, as before stated. This has fixed and intensified the qualities, and at the same time secured the greatest possible uniformity and really established a breed, separate and distinct from all others. This is the way in which all the valuable breeds have been established, and this **is the** first persistent and successful effort at establishing a purely American breed that has ever been made. While carefully watching results and selecting for breeding purposes, **Mr.** Cole has steadily **refused** to be turned from his course, or to change his purpose of establishing a uniform butter breed, and of testing the fallacy of the popular notion about the injurious effects of inbreeding. His thirty years of the closest inbreeding have shown no such disastrous effects, but, **on** the contrary, have produced only good ones. There **is** no failure **in** form or constitution. The only marked external change, save in securing the greatest uniformity, has been in the gradual change of color. The original animals were pale red and white, the white being along **the** back from the shoulders to the tail, down the hind-quar-

American Holderness Bull, LEWIS F. ALLEN,
at 16 months.
Property of T. A. Cole, Solsville, N. Y.

American Holderness Cow, ADELAIDE 17th.
Property of T. A. Cole, Solsville, N. Y.

ters, and along the belly to the shoulders. This distribution of the light and dark colors has remained essentially the same, but the light red gradually turned to dark red, then to brindle and finally to black. The later bred animals are all black and white. But the calves, when first dropped, are still red and white, the red changing to black when the first coat of hair is shed. This is probably one of the most remarkable cases of inbreeding on record, as the breed is also one of the most remarkable. All who have tried this stock are remarkably well pleased with it, and calves readily sell for $100 a head with a demand greater than the supply—and this without any newspaper advertising. The breed is endorsed by Mr. Lewis F. Allen, former editor of the Shorthorn Herd-Book, and author of a work on cattle that stands second to none as authority. This endorsement has appeared in print over Mr. Allen's signature, as have the favorable opinions of many other good judges. In the latest edition of his book on the Cattle of America, he says:

"I never saw a more uniform herd of cows, in their general appearance and excellence, which latter quality they daily prove in the milk they produce. * * Compared with ordinary dairy herds, the uniformity in yield testifies to their purity of breeding and management."

Col. Weld, who saw these cattle on exhibition at the New York State Fair, held at Utica in 1879, said of them, in the November number of the *American Agriculturist;*

"The cattle of this 'Cole-Holderness breed' are of good size and fair form as beef animals. * * * They are deep-bodied, with large udders and teats, with excellent escutcheons, great swollen and tortuous milk-veins and skins as yellow as Guernsey's. The interior of their ears was almost like orange-peel. **The butter** made from their milk * * * showed admirable color and keeping qualities. * * * Could we test the various breeds of cattle, with the view of determining with accuracy which is the most profitable dairy cow for all purposes—butter, cheese, veal, and ultimately beef—giving to each its fair weight in the scale of excellence, I would not be surprised if Mr. Cole's breed would win the distinction of being the most useful of all."

INBREEDING.

A word here about inbreeding will not be out of place. It may be disastrous, or it may be beneficial. So **also** may be crossing or grading. The evil as well as the good qualities are developed and intensified. Like begets like. Couple animals having **the same bad** points, and these points will be increased and strengthened. Couple those with good points, and corresponding results follow—that is, the good are increased and strengthened. But if one animal has one point to excess, so as to become a deformity, and the other is deformed by lack of this same point, it is both safe and advantageous to breed them together, as the result is likely to be a medium between the two. So, whatever the manner of breeding—inbreeding, crossing or grading—the good or evil results depend altogether on the characteristics of the animals **coupled**. Inbreeding intensifies and fixes the **qualities, be** they good or bad.

SWISS.

There have been a few importations of Swiss cattle, which are short-legged and strong-boned, and hence well adapted to hilly regions. Some of these have made splendid butter records—from 500 to over 700 pounds of butter in a year. We should have great hopes of them for the mountainous sections of our country; but as yet importation and breeding of this stock is not extensive enough to permit of their availability to any considerable extent for dairy purposes.

POLLED.

The polled or hornless cattle are great favorites with some of the Western people, and an effort is made to get up a boom on them. But they not only lack in numbers, but in the essential quality of a large flow of milk, or of a very rich one. The best information we can get does not indicate usefulness for the dairy. Neither do they excel several of the other breeds for beef. Their chief recommend appears to be their destitution of horns, which in our eye is far from a mark of beauty. It gives them a sort of bald, unfinished look that is anything but pleasing. We prefer, for looks, short, well-turned horns. But of course, without horns there is no hooking, but pushing is by no means avoided. Besides, in some cases we have known a lack of horns to make it difficult to fasten the animals in stanchions or with ropes. This may not be true of the cows; but we were cognizant of an instance on the New York State Fair grounds where a polled bull was constantly getting loose. His neck was so thick that he could slip his head through any place not tight enough to choke him. As to disposition, we presume the lack of horns would not make the bulls any more amiable. However, we have nothing to say against this kind of stock, and would advise all who like them to keep them. If horns are objectionable, it is easy to prevent them from growing on any stock by removing the first appearance of them on the calf. This can be done without much pain to the calf and without much trouble to one who knows how to do it. It, as we understand, requires no great skill, and can hardly be said to come under the head of cruelty to animals. It is nothing like as painful as castration.

HEREFORDS.

The Herefords are having quite a boom in the West, but it is not as dairy stock, but as superior for beef. We have seen no strong claims put in for them for dairy purposes. The few we have seen did not seem to indicate any great dairy qualities, nor have any of the numerous portraits we have seen published borne the marks of dairy stock. But the claim of beef qualities we believe is well founded. Their great rivals in this line are the Shorthorns.

COMMON STOCK.

We have not mentioned the so-called "Native" stock as a dairy breed, because it is not a breed, but a mixture of breeds—crazy-quilt stock. We would not be understood as considering it of no value for dairy purposes, for when carefully selected, a dairy herd of commonn stock may be very valuable. Great milkers and great butter makers are not uncommon among them; but there is such a mixture of blood in their veins that there is no guarantee of their producing their like. They originally sprang from the best animals that the early emigrants could select to bring over with them from Europe. But they were subsequently cross-bred so promiscuously that no trace of the original blood can be discovered with any certainty. They were also subjected to great exposure and hardship, with scanty food, which had a greatly deteriorating tendency. But, perhaps worst of all, there was no careful selection of males for breeding purposes, nor any attempt at judicious coupling for improvement, or for even the maintenance of the existing status. In short, the entire treatment and all the surroundings had a deteriorating influence and a tendency to the production of scrubs. If we were to take all the existing pure-blood stock and breed it together promiscuously, while at the same time subjecting it to harsh treatment and neglect, it would not require a very long period to reduce it to the same mongrel and scrub condition in which we now find the common stock of the country. Yet some of **our** common stock make excellent crosses, when pure-**blood males** are used. But no improvement or valuable results could come from using common stock bulls **on** pure-blood or other cows. The male has the controlling influence, and to the constant use of pure-blood males must we look for the improvement of the common stock of the country and for the maintenance of the existing status of the pure-bloods; and not only must we use pure-blood males, but keep up a constant and careful selection of the best. Neither should we trust to cross-bred or grade bulls for breeding purposes; for the progeny will inherit the traits of ancestors on one side or the other, and hence will lack in uniformity, both in appearance and in quality. When we use a grade bull, the result is just the opposite of what it is when we use a pure blood. With the latter, we get half-bloods, then quarter, then eighths, sixteenths, thirty-seconds, and so on. toward pure blood; **but with** a half-blood grade bull, the first offspring from common stock has only one-fourth pure blood, the next cross has only one-eighth, the third one-sixteenth pure blood, and so on—reducing the purity in the same ratio as the use of pure blood improves it—if we continue to breed from the grade male offspring. If we always use a half-blood male, there may be a slight improvement in the blood. But the improvement is too slow and the benefit too uncertain to make the use of a grade bull advisable when a pure blood can be had.

BREEDING DAIRY STOCK.

HAVING briefly glanced at the characteristics of the different breeds, it will not be out of place to say a few words about breeding and rearing dairy stock. There are three things to be considered:

1. Selection.
2. Coupling.
3. Care.

SELECTION.

By selection, we mean not only the selection of the breed adapted to the line of dairying pursued, but the selection of the individual animals to breed and rear animals from, and especially the bull to be used on the herd. This male should have a good pedigree—that is, be the lineal descendant of animals known to possess the qualities desired in the future herd. This is all-important; for however well-formed and comely he may be, he will transmit the qualities of his ancestors as surely as like begets like. This fact can never be safely ignored. Milk and butter qualities, in a dairy herd, must take precedence over beauty of form, however desirable the latter may be. The cows to rear stock from should be selected, as far as possible, on the same principle. Pedigree is not of as much consequence in a cow, so far as practical results are concerned, though it helps insure certainty in the quality of the offspring when that of the cow, as well as of the bull, is right. But we may safely venture on raising the calves of a good milker, as the probabilities are that the offspring will inherit the qualities of the sire, while it may also inherit the qualities of the dam, though she be of the most mongrel or mixed blood. If there is failure, however, it need not go beyond that one animal—unless an attempt is made to use a grade bull on a nondescript dam, in which case prepotency is weakened and mongrelism may show in the offspring. But grade bulls should never be used when it is possible to have the use of the right kind of pure blood, which is always stronger than mixed blood, and hence a pure blood sire is pretty sure to transmit the qualities of his herd and family, in a great degree, even when coupled with a cow of uncertain blood. In breeding, the one bull makes half the herd, and when used on common stock, the offspring will always be half-bloods the first generation. The second generation they become three-quarter bloods; the third seven eighths; the fourth fifteen-sixteenth, and so on, constantly approaching, but **never** reaching, purity. For all dairy purposes, **however, they** become practically as good as pure-bloods. But if the breeding is the other way—that is, if a scrub bull is used on pure-blood cows—the degeneration to the scrub status is in precisely the same ratio that we have just given for improvement when pure-blood males are constantly used. By using grade bulls, there is also a constant deteriora-

BREEDING DAIRY STOCK. 37

tion of blood, but not as rapid as when **scrub bulls are** used. The only safety is in using pure **blood males.** With these well selected and **all** other **conditions maintained,** the status is certain to **be preserved, if improvements,** in consequence of better **care and selection, are** not secured

COUPLING.

Proper coupling, or rather the coupling of proper **animals, has** received little attention, and is now confined **generally if** not exclusively to professional breeders. **But it is** a subject to which the dairymen can **as** well as **not** pay attention with good results. By coupling proper animals, we mean having **regard to** individual points and qualities, never **coupling those having the same defects,** either in form **or quality. For,** instance, **to illustrate, a cow high on the rump** may be safely bred to **a** bull low on the rump, or *vice versa*, the result, in all probability, being an offspring with a level rump. This is breeding together opposite extremes, depending on the one to correct the other. But if we breed two sloped rumps together, or two humped rumps, the **result** would be to exaggerate and intensify or strengthen this deformity in the offspring. So of quality or disposition. **A** nervous cow bred to a nervous or irritable bull, would be pretty sure to drop a calf that would be more nervous than either sire or dam. But if one of the parents is dull and sluggish and the other irritable and sensitive, the offspring might be an improvement on both. Again, a **cow** lacking in the quality of richness of milk, though **giving a large** flow, should not be coupled with a bull

descended from a family having the same peculiarity of
large flow lacking in richness. But if there is richness
on one side and abundance on the other, the coupling of
the two might reasonably be expected to result in improvement in the offspring, which might inherit both the
large flow and the rich quality. Bad points and qualities
are inherited as well as good ones. Hence, the constant
aim and care must be to avoid developing what is objectionable as well as to develop what is desired. It must
be constantly borne in mind that like begets like. All
the trouble attending inbreeding, crossing or grading
comes from not properly regarding this fact. Where
inbreeding is followed, the only disadvantage arises from
the fact that all the animals are likely to have the same
defects of form, quality and constitution. But where
these are all right, the advantage is that inbreeding fixes
the features and qualities and secures the establishment
of them in a type **or** breed. But crossing or grading
animals having the same failing will prove just **as** disastrous as would inbreeding. But crossing may be done in
a way to develop good qualities, and these may afterward
be fixed by careful selection and inbreeding of offspring.
This subject of breeding is one of great importance,
and yet little understood. Many things pertaining **to it**
are yet to be settled, though great progress has been
made during the last few years, and public attention is
being drawn to it as it never **was** before. It will be
found that man can become master of the situation, and
may, by observing certain fundamental conditions and
varying only the details, breed domestic animals of

almost any form, disposition, and quality, **that he may** desire.

CARE AND KEEP.

Better care and keep, however, are the key notes to improvement. Higher conditions and better surroundings lead to improvements which may be developed into fixed traits by proper selection and coupling, provided the improved environment is maintained. The status can be maintained only by maintaining the conditions. This is what we mean by care. Under this head, **we** include all that pertains to the health and comfort of the animal. Judicious care is of prime importance not only in breeding but in securing the best results in dairy products. Proper food and drink and enough of it, with shelter, kind treatment, regularity and the most thorough system, must be provided, or corresponding failure, for any and all abuse, neglect or mistake, is sure to follow.

FEEDING STOCK.

THE question of feeding stock is yearly rising into greater prominence and importance. Formerly, it was thought that anybody who could throw out coarse fodder and hay to cattle knew enough for all practical purposes about feeding, and **that** any sort of a shelter, or no shelter, if the animal survived, was sufficient. Better ideas are beginning to prevail. Few men now think they know all that can be learned about feeding stock, and those who know the most are the most anxious to learn. A thorough knowledge of feeding requires a knowledge of physiology and biology, with the chemical composition and nutritive qualities of the different kinds of food. Added to this must be the practical knowledge gained by observation of the effects of the different foods on different animals under various conditions. And when all is known that can be, there will still be room left for the exercise of the best judgment of the feeder **as to the** conditions and requirements of the animal **fed**, and as to the quality of the foods available **and the** quantity and proportions of each.

CARBONACEOUS AND NITROGENOUS FOODS.

It is pretty well known what the constituents of the animal organism are, and what elements of nutrition are required in the food for the sustenance of **the animal**. Of these primal elements—some twelve **or fifteen in** number—it is found that, practically, when foods combined contain two of them in proper proportion, the rest **are** generally present in sufficient quantity. These two are CARBON and NITROGEN, **and** the foods containing them in relatively large **proportion** are respectively called *carbonaceous* and *nitrogenous*. All foods contain these elements in **greater or** less proportion. The proper proportion for feeding **is** found to be about *one* **of** nitrogen to *five* or *six* of carbon. If the temperature of the weather **is low,** the proportion of carbon **may** be **raised to** eight, **and** even ten, where little exercise **is had—as, for** instance, milch cows standing **in a** cold stable. **But, in** hot weather, when cows **are giving milk,** the carbon may be reduced to four **and** even three—that is, so that there shall be one **part** of nitrogen to three or four parts of carbon. The carbon is heat and fat producing, and some class it as motor producing, but we think this is a mistake, save so far as heat is essential to motion. We think **nitrogen** is motor producing as well as muscle producing —or, in **other** words, that the element which produces the organs of motion also fills them with energy, for the exercise of which heat **is essential.** **We** cannot have motion, or even life, **much below the** normal temperature of about 98 degrees Fahrenheit. At all events, it **is** found necessary to feed nitrogenous food to all animals that are working hard, to supply the waste of muscle—and we think also to replace the expended energy. Dr. J. Milner Fothergill, in his work on the "Maintenance of

Health," published by G. P. Putnam's Sons, says : " The effect of the nitrogen upon the brain is to *evolve nerve force freely*, and this rules and regulates the actual force which takes its origin in the respiratory foods consumed. These respiratory foods furnish the force itself, but the nitrogenized foods furnish the manifesters of force." It appears to us that the nerve force, which he says is evolved, is all there is of it, save the requisite conditions afforded by heat. Dr. Houghton says : "The hunted deer will outrun the leopard in a fair open chase, because the force supplied to its muscles by vegetable food is capable of being given out continuously for a long period of time; but in a sudden rush at a near distance, the leopard will infallibly overtake the deer, because its flesh food stores up in the blood a reserve of force capable of being given out instantaneously in the form of exceedingly swift muscualr action." Dr. Fothergill goes on to say: " Nitrogen is the essential factor in all explosive compounds, from gunpowder to nerve force. It endows the consumer of it with energy and **enables** him to discharge his force quickly and rapidly." Again, he says of the race-horse : "His food affects his speed and endurance, and without his nitrogenized food he would cut a poor figure at a race, because without it he could not discharge his force fast enough."

WHAT IS CARBON?

It is pure in the diamond, nearly pure in coal, and is the principal constituent of all woody fiber—also of oils, fat, starch, sugar, etc. Nearly all the visible organic world is composed of carbon. It appears to be very plentiful, but of our atmosphere it composes only about four-ten-thousandths, while oxygen, with which it unites to form carbonic acid gas for vegetation to feed on, composes one-fifth and nitrogen four-fifths. Really, we have little trouble in securing carbonaceous foods. The only difficulty is to get them in a digestible form. Only what is soluble can be digested and assimilated by the animal organism. Hence, great care must be taken to get food in a proper condition for animal nutrition.

WHAT IS NITROGEN?

It is almost pure in the albumens, both vegetable and animal. It is nearly pure in the white of egg. Hence, nitrogenous foods are quite commonly called albuminoids. It exists abundantly in all the proteins—as cheese or caseine, fibrin or lean meat, albumen, etc. Nitrogen, in its free state, appears to be an innocuous gas, diluting the oxygen and preventing it from rapidly oxydizing or burning up everything. As before said, it constitutes four-fifths of our atmosphere, but does not appear to be directly appropriated by either vegetables or animals. As food for either, it must be in combination with other elements—especially carbon—and yet it is very difficult to make it unite with other elements, and hard to maintain the union when it is once formed. Its disposition is to break these unions and seek an idle state of freedom. Hence it is that, when held in durance, its constant tendency to free itself makes it the motor force in all animal organisms, and the terrible energy in all explosives. It is secured in the form of ammonia in rain, by a process called nitrification it unites with the soil, and it exists in all decayed animal and vegetable matter in a form suitable for plant food. Men and animals get it by eating vegetables or by eating one another. It is a very abundant and important element, yet very difficult to obtain in an available form for plant and animal food. Fortunately, but comparatively little of it is needed.

COMPOUNDING RATIONS.

By referring to the feed tables furnished by the analysts of this country and Europe, the farmer can learn the constituents of foods. Then, knowing the ration required, he can take different foods and compound in the right proportions aimed at in feeding, whether for work, for growth, for fat, for bare maintenance, or for milk. We give the German standards for feeding animals:

FEEDING STOCK.

PER DAY AND PER 1,000 LBS. LIVE WEIGHT.

ANIMALS.	Total organic dry substance.	Nutritive digestible sub.			Total nutritive sub.	Nutritive ratio.
		Albuminoids.	Carbohydrates.	Fat.		
	lbs.	lbs.	lbs.	lbs.	lbs.	lbs.
1. Oxen at rest in stall	17.5	0.7	8.0	0.15	8.85	1:12
2. Oxen moderately worked	24.0	1.6	11.3	0.30	13.20	1:7.5
3. Oxen heavily worked	26.0	2.4	13.2	0.50	16.10	1:6.0
4. Oxen fattening, 1st period	27.0	2.5	15.0	0.50	18.00	1:6.5
4. Oxen fattening, 2d period	26.0	3.0	14.8	0.70	18.50	1:5.5
4. Oxen fattening, 3d period	25.0	2.7	14.8	0.60	18.10	1:6.0
5. Cows in milk	24.0	2.5	12.5	0.40	15.40	1:5.4

GROWING CATTLE—PER DAY AND PER HEAD.

Age. Months.	Average live weight per head.					
2 to 3	150 pounds	3.3	0.6	2.1	0.30	3.00	1:4.7
3 to 6	300 pounds	7.0	1.0	4.1	0.30	5.40	1:5.0
6 to 12	500 pounds	12.0	1.3	6.8	0.30	8.40	1:6.0
12 to 18	700 pounds	16.8	1.4	9.1	0.28	10.78	1:7.0
18 to 24	850 pounds	20.4	1.4	12.3	0.26	11.96	1:8.0

SAMPLE RATIONS.

Dr. Wolf gives an illustration of the standard for a milch cow, by saying that 30 lbs. of young clover hay will keep a cow in good milk; and that this contains of dry organic substance, 23 lbs., of which is digestible—albuminoids 3.21, carbohydrates 11.28, and fat 0.63. This is .71 lb. albuminoids more, and .22 lb. of carbohydrates less, with .13 lb. of fat more, than the standard. Then he takes the richest and best meadow hay, of which 30 lbs. contains of organic substance 23.2 lbs., having digestible —albuminoids 2.49 lbs., carbohydrates 12.75 lbs., and fat 42 lb. This is almost exactly the feeding standard.

As will have been seen by what has preceded, the German standard ration for a milch cow is 24 lbs. of dry organic substance, containing 2.50 lbs. nitrogenous food, and 12.90 lbs. of carbonaceous food. To secure this, Dr. Wolff recommends for every 1,000 lbs of live weight:

    12 lbs. average meadow hay.
    6 " oat straw.
    20 " mangolds.
    25 " brewers' grain.
    2 " cotton seed cake.

Prof. S. W. Johnson's ration for the same purpose is:

    20 lbs. corn fodder.
    5 " rye straw.
    6 " malt sprouts.
    2 " cotton seed meal.

The following milk rations are recommended by Prof. E. W. Stewart:

FEEDING STOCK.

No. 1.
18 lbs. oat straw.
5 " bean straw.
6 " cotton seed cake.

No. 2.
20 lbs. barley straw.
5 " pea straw.
2 " wheat bran.
5 " linseed meal.

No. 3.
20 lbs. poor hay.
5 " corn meal.
5 " cotton seed cake.

No. 4.
20 lbs. wheat straw.
5 " wheat bran.
3 " corn meal.
4 " linseed meal.

No. 5.
20 lbs. fresh marsh hay.
5 " corn meal.
5 " cotton seed meal.

No. 6.
10 lbs. good mead'w hay.
10 " rye straw.
3 " wheat bran.
5 " linseed meal.

The following are given by the same author as milk rations:

No. 1.
10 lbs. clover hay.
10 " straw.
4 " linseed oil **cake.**
4 " wheat bran.
2 " cotton seed cake.
4 " corn meal.

No. 2.
16 lbs. meadow hay.
8 " wheat bran.
2 " linseed meal.
6 " corn meal.

No. 3.
18 lbs. corn fodder.
8 "wheat bran.
4 " cotton seed meal.
4 " corn meal.

No, 4.
15 **lbs.** straw.
5 " hay.
4 " cotton seed meal
4 " bran.
4 " corn meal.
3 " malt sprouts.

No. 5.
10 lbs. corn fodder.
10 " oat straw.
2 " linseed meal.
4 " malt sprouts.
10 " oat & corn meal.

No. 6.
60 lbs corn ensilage.
5 " hay.
2 " linseed meal.
4 " bran.

FATTENING RATIONS.

The following rations are recommended by Prof. E. W. Stewart for fattening cattle. The rations are for 1,000 pounds of live weight:

No. 1.
18 lbs. wint'r wh't straw.
40 " corn sugar meal.
4 " cotton seed meal.

No. 2.
12 lbs oat straw.
10 " wheat bran.
40 " corn sugar meal.

No. 3.
12 lbs. clover hay.
6 " oat straw.
40 " corn sugar meal.
2 " linseed meal.

No. 4.
15 lbs. corn fodder.
5 " malt sprouts.
3 " corn meal.
40 " corn sugar meal.

No. 5.
20 lbs. best clover hay.
50 " corn sugar meal.

No. 6.
20 lbs. wheat straw.
8 " timothy hay.
6 " cotton seed cake

No. 7.
20 lbs. corn fodder.
6 " Indian corn.
6 " linseed cake.

WORKING RATIONS.

The following are rations for **oxen at hard** work, as given by Prof. Stewart:

No. 1.
20 lbs. best meadow hay.
10 " corn meal.

No. 2.
20 lbs. corn fodder.
5 " clover hay.
2 " wheat bran.
3 " cotton seed cake.

No. 3.
17 lbs. clover hay.
3 " wheat bran.
10 " corn meal.

No. 4.
25 lbs. oat straw.
5 " wheat bran.
4 " linseed cake.

DIGESTIBILITY OF FOODS.

The following table, copied from Prof. Stewart, gives the digestibility of a few of the more common foods:

CLOVER HAY.

	In 100 lbs.	Digestible.	Digestible In 2,000 lbs.
Albuminoids	15.3	10.7	214
Carbo-hydrates	35.8 }	37.5	752
Crude fibre	22.2 }		
Fat	3.2	2.1	42
			1008

FEEDING STOCK.

	In 100 lbs.	Digestible.	Digestible in 2,000 lbs.
AVERAGE MEADOW HAY.			
Albuminoids	9.7	5.4	108
Carbo-hydrates	41.6	41.0	820
Crude fiber	21.9		
Fat	2.5	1.0	20
			948
CORN FODDER.			
Albuminoids	4.4	3.2	66
Carbo hydrates	37.9	43.4	868
Crude fiber	25.0		
Fat	1.3	1.0	20
			954
OAT STRAW.			
Albuminoids	4.0	1.4	28
Carbo-hydrates	36.2	40.1	802
Crude fibre	39.5		
Fat	2.0	0.7	14
			844
LINSEED OIL CAKE.			
Albuminoids	28.3	23.77	475
Carbo-hydrates	32.3	35.15	703
Fibre	10.0		
Fat	10.0	9.0	180
			1358
WHEAT BRAN.			
Albuminoids	15.0	12.9	252
Carbo-hydrates	52.2	42.6	852
Fibre	10.1		
Fat	3.2	2.6	52
			1156
CORN MEAL.			
Albuminoids	10.0	8.4	168
Carbo-hydrates	62.1	60.6	1212
Crude fibre	5.5		
Fat	6.5	4.8	96
			1476
OATS.			
Albuminoids	12.0	9.0	180
Carbo-hydrates	55.0	43.0	860
Crude fibre	9.3		
Fat	6.5	4.7	94
			1134

ELEMENTS OF FOOD.

We give the names of a few foods, with their relative amount of nitrogenous and carbonaceous elements:

FOODS.	Nitrogenous.	Carbonaceous.	FOODS.	Nitrogenous.	Carbonaceous.
Meadow hay, medium	1 to	8.0	Potatoes	1 to	10.6
Red clover, medium	1 "	5.9	Artichokes	1 "	8.7
Lucerne, good	1 "	2.8	Ruttabagas	1 "	8.3
Swedish clover (alsike)	1 "	4.9	Sugar beets	1 "	17.0
Orchard grass, in blos'm	1 "	6.5	Carrots	1 "	9.3
White clover, medium	1 "	5.0	Turnips	1 "	5.8
Timothy	1 "	8.1	Wheat, grain	1 "	5.8
Blue grass, in blossom	1 "	7.5	Rye, grain	1 "	7.0
Red top	1 "	5.4	Barley, grain	1 "	7.9
Fodder rye	1 "	7.2	Oats, grain	1 "	6.1
Italian rye grass	1 "	6.3	Maize, grain	1 "	8.6
Hungarian grass	1 "	7.1	Millet, grain	1 "	5.4
Rich pasture grass	1 "	3.6	Peas, grain	1 "	2.9
Green maize, German	1 "	8.9	Buckwheat, grain	1 "	7.4
Fodder oats	1 "	7.2	Cotton seed	1 "	4.6
Sorghum	1 "	7.4	Pumpkins	1 "	18.4
Pasture clover, young	1 "	2.5	Coarse wheat bran	1 "	5.6
Red clover, before bl's'm	1 "	3.8	Wheat middlings	1 "	6.9
Red clover, in blossom	1 "	5.7	Rye bran	1 "	5.3
White clover, in blossom	1 "	4.2	Barley bran	1 "	4.5
Buckwheat, in blossom	1 "	5.1	Buckwheat bran	1 "	4.1
Fodder cabbage	1 "	5.2	Hempseed cake	1 "	1.5
Ruttabaga leaves	1 "	3.9	Sunflower	1 "	1.3
Fermented hay, from maize	1 "	12.0	Corn bran	1 "	10.3
			Brewers' grain	1 "	3.0
Fermented hay, from beet leaves	1 "	4.0	Malt sprouts	1 "	2.2
			Wheat meal	1 "	5.7
Fermented hay, from red clover	1 "	4.1	Rape cake	1 "	1.7
			Rape meal, extracted	1 "	1.3
Winter wheat straw	1 "	45.8	Barley, middlings	1 "	6.0
Winter rye straw	1 "	52.0	Oat bran	1 "	9.7
Winter barley straw	1 "	40.5	Linseed cake	1 "	2.0
Oat straw	1 "	29.9	Linseed meal, extracted	1 "	1.4
Corn stalks	1 "	34.4	Cot'n-seed meal, decort.	1 "	1.8
Seed clover	1 "	7.4	Cot'n-s'd cake, undecort.	1 "	1.7
Wheat chaff	1 "	24.1	Cow's milk	1 "	4.4
Rye chaff	1 "	32.6	Buttermilk	1 "	2.6
Oat chaff	1 "	23.8	Skimmed milk	1 "	1.9
Barley chaff	1 "	30.4	Cream	1 "	30.5

FEEDING STOCK.

ENSILAGE.

Major Henry E. Alvord, of Houghton Farm, N. Y., gives the following as the range and average of analyses by a large number of eminent scientists:

	Range in 100 lbs.	Average.
Total dry matter	15.10 to 25.90	18.60
Water	84.90 to 74.10	81.40
Protein	0.90 to 1.90	1.30
Fat	0.30 to 0.90	0.60
Nitrogen-free extract	7.60 to 13.40	9.60
Crude Fiber	4.70 to 7.90	5.90
Ash	0.90 to 1.40	1.20

REMARKS.

It is safe to always feed cotton seed meal, bran, or linseed cake with corn fodder, **or** fodder corn, or ensilage. And it will always be found to work well if corn meal is fed with clover hay. **Corn ensilage** with clover hay will constitute a proper feed. To avoid waste, and secure the best results, we must learn to balance the nitrogenous and carbonaceous foods. Our greatest difficulty in feeding, as in manuring the soil, is to secure enough of the nitrogenous elements. These are what we have mainly to look out for, the carbonaceous foods usually being over abundant.

Not only must we proportion the elements of food properly, but we must prepare the food so that it will be in a proper condition. It may contain all the elements, but in consequence of being in a bad or wrong condition, the animal cannot digest it. There is plenty of carbon in coal, but who would expect the animal stomach to digest it? So there is nitrogen in saltpeter and gun-cotton, but they are not in a suitable condition **or** form for digestion, and hence have no food value. Most raw vegetables are indigestible in the human stomach, but cook them, and thus put them in a proper condition, and they become nutritious foods.

There are few, if any, perfect foods. Every food needs to be supplemented with something else. Hence it is that both men and animals want variety. Summer pasture, composed of mixed grasses, makes the best food for all kinds of stock. Meadow hay, cut at the right time and properly cured—provided there is a mixture of grasses—makes a proper food for winter; but even this needs to be accompanied by roots, ensilage or something of a juicy nature, as a relish, if for nothing else, and as an aid to digestion.

In a state of nature, roaming free, animals select and balance their rations according to the cravings of appetite. But when domesticated, they have no such freedom of choice, except perhaps in a few of the summer months. In winter, they must take what is given to them. It is our duty, therefore, to give their food a proper balance of elements as far as possible; and in thus conforming to the laws of nature, we shall find both the greatest economy and the greatest profit.

HANDLING MILK.

IT is a comparatively easy operation to milk, if one knows how. The process is about as simple as that of Columbus in making an egg stand on end, but it requires skill, practice and a muscular hand to do it well. Grasping the teat so as to fill it with milk, and then tighten the thumb and fore finger so as to prevent a return of the milk to the udder as the rest of the fingers are gently but firmly closed, so as to give a downward pressure and expel the milk, is not likely to be done by the novice the first time trying. But ordinarily, the performance of this operation is soon achieved by any one who wishes to learn, though it is declared by some that they "never could learn to milk." Substitute "would" for "could," and we think the truth is more nearly approximated. Still there is a great difference in milkers, as well as in cows, the man or woman with a good grip in the hand having decidedly the advantage, both as regards ease and expedition—and it is quite important that the milk should all be quickly and continuously drawn from the cow after the milking is begun, and while the cow is in the mood of " giving down."

KEEP QUIET.

If a cow is suddenly disturbed, so as to get excited, or gets tired and out of patience, the flow of milk may be prematurely stopped. If this disturbance is continued from time to time, the effect will be to permanently lessen the flow, or "dry up" the cow. Anything that irritates a cow, while being milked, reduces both quality and quantity. Hence, milking should be done in a quiet and orderly manner. Treat the cow very kindly and gently, so as to gain her confidence, and be as careful as possible not to hurt her teats by unnecessarily tearing open any cracks there may be, or pinching any warts, and be sure to not dig your finger-nails into the teats.

REGULARITY.

It is a good plan to milk cows regularly in the same order, taking the same one first, and winding up with the same one every time. Regularity of hour in commencing the milking of the herd is an advantange in securing the best results, since animals as well as men are greatly the creatures of habit, and when the time comes around the cow will desire to be milked and all the functions of her system will concur in this desire.

KEEP DOWN THE FOUL ODORS.

The milking should be done in a sweet, clean place—either a stable kept scrupulously clean, and plaster or other deoderizer freely used, or in a row of stanchions in an open shed, with barely a roof to keep off storm and sunshine, and no filthy deposits allowed to accumulate

HANDLING MILK. 55

around, it. The milk, as fast as drawn, **should be removed** from the place of milking, **lest** it absorb **odors** from the droppings, the breath, or the exhalations from the cow's body—or even from the sweat and grime of the person and clothes of the milker—for milk is extremely sensitive to these influences. It is much more so than is popularly supposed, and should be put in a sweet atmosphere as soon as possible when drawn. Fine fancy goods, with the most delicious and delicate flavor, cannot be made from milk that has been exposed to the influence of a foul atmosphere.

KEEP OUT THE DIRT.

So, also, great care should be taken to keep out all hairs, dirt and filth of every kind. If permitted to get into the milk, filth cannot be entirely strained out, and hence some of its odors and flavors will linger in the fats of the milk and appear in the product manufactured from it. The indispensable necessity for clean utensils has already been mentioned. Filth from this source will not only affect odor and flavor, but is quite likely to contain the germs of ferment which will multiply in the milk and product, and cause disastrous results. With a clean can, clean pails and clean hands, begin the task of milking by brushing off all loose materials from the cow's side that may rattle down into the pail, carefully brush and clean the udder and teats, and then place the pail between your knees in a way to prevent the cow putting her foot into it, or upsetting it, if she should move about nervously, or be suddenly startled—which should not be permitted if it is possible to avoid it.

LET OUT THE COWS.

As fast as milked, it is best to let the cows go. This gives more room, reduces the generation of heat in the stable or milking place, and lessens the amount of droppings and consequent bad odors rising from them. Those left will soon understand this and not get uneasy.

A LICK OF MEAL.

If the cows have been prepared for milking by giving them a lick of meal, or a little dry hay, when they come into the stable, it will be found to have a good effect. It will also cultivate a willingness to come home at milking time and take their respective places in the stanchions. It pays to please and satisfy a cow. She will deposit her appreciation in the pail.

CARE OF MILK.

When the milking is over, the milk should **be taken** as directly to the place of manufacture as possible. **If it** must be kept over night, see that it is well **stirred** and properly cooled to 70 degrees Fahrenheit, before leaving it. Do not put on a close cover, unless the milk is thoroughly cooled. It is far better to deliver it directly to the cheese or butter maker, who knows how to care for it, and has facilities for doing the work—or, **at least,** ought to have. Very much depends on **having** the **milk** delivered in good condition. If it **is not, no** after care and skill can make a perfect **product** from it. True, if all right when delivered, it may **be** afterward injured or spoiled, but it is not likely to be. It is therefore the duty of the patron to do his part of the work all right; then

HANDLING MILK.   57

he may with some reason blame the operator if the result is not right. But butter and cheese makers are too often expected to turn out first-class products from second or third class milk—a task impossible to perform. With good milk and proper facilities, there is no valid excuse for failure.

The first object is the production of good milk. This is of prime importance. Without it, the after product must of necessity be inferior. The next object is to preserve the milk in its best condition, all through the handling, in order to reach the best results. Milk is often spoiled in the handling. **Hence** care and judgment must be exercised to maintain **the** proper conditions to the end.

COMPOSITION OF MILK.

Few understand the delicate and complex nature of milk. It is a compound of many ingredients; and if any one of these is disturbed, it affects the whole. Their union **is** very weak and unstable, and liable to be broken by **many** influences. To give a clearer idea of the composition of milk, we copy the following diagram, prepared by Dr. E. Lewis Sturtevant, Director of the New York Agricultural Experiment Station:

MILK.

- **Cream.**
  - **Butter.**
    - Solid Fat.
      - Stearin
      - Palmatin
    - Liquid Fat.
      - Olein
      - Butyrin
      - Caproin
      - Caprylin
      - Caprin
      - Aracin
      - *Myristin.
  - **Butter Milk.**
    - Casein.
    - Whey or Serum.
- **Skim Milk.**
  - **Coag'ble Matter.**
    - By Rennet. Casein.
    - By Acetic Acid. †Ziega.
  - **Whey or Serum.**
    - Salts.
      - Potash
      - Soda
      - Lime
      - Magnesia
      - Iron
      - Sulph. Acid
      - Phos. Acid
      - Carbonic Acid
      - Silicic Acid
      - Chlorine.
    - Nitrog. Matter or Osmazome
    - Sach. Matter or Milk Sugar.

*Not found in all milk.
†Includes, albumen and whatever else is coagulable by acetic acid.

HANDLING MILK. 59

Here are between twenty and thirty different constituents, in various proportions. Their combination is effected through the organism of the cow, the ultimate work being performed by the udder, where it is no sooner completed than reaction **begins** and change is the result.

DETERIORATION OF MILK IN THE UDDER.

The longer the milk remains in the udder, the more it is impoverished by absorption of some of its ingredients. This is specially true of the fats, which are taken up by the absorbent vessels of the udder and carried into general circulation. For this reason, the first milk drawn—which is the first secreted, and therefore remains in the udder the longest—is the poorest milk drawn, and that which is last secreted and last milked (the strippings) is the richest. Hence, the longer the interval between milkings, the poorer the milk for butter making. Three milkings a day will give better results than two.

DO FATS EXPAND BEFORE CONGEALING?

If milk is to be set for cream, the sooner it is put to rest and the less **heat** it looses before setting, the better for the separation of the cream. If cooled down much, the cream will rise more slowly and separate more imperfectly. In cooling, the fluids and semi-fluids condense faster than the fats, and hence become relatively heavier, and settle as the fat globules rise, by virtue of the law of gravitation. The theory has been broached by Mr. H. B. Gurler, of DeKalb, Illinois, that in sudden cooling, the fluids and semi-fluids are not only condensed, but the fats expanded, thus increasing the difference in specific gravity in both directions. In this way, the rapid rising of cream in sudden cooling he thinks may be better accounted for. His idea is based on the fact that water, just before congealing, begins to expand and continues to expand as the temperature lowers. Fats consolidate at a much higher temperature than water, and he thinks the same law of expansion may intervene in both cases. So far as we are aware, it is not known whether fats **do actually** expand before and after reaching the point of congelation or not, and we shall feel an interest in having the question positively settled by the scientists. If it is a fact, it introduces a new element into our philosophy, and will help in the solution of some points not yet satisfactorily determined.

EFFECTS OF FALLING TEMPERATURE.

It is a fact that cream rises best in a falling temperature, very slowly in a stationary one, and little or none in a rising temperature. Hence, in cold weather, when milk cools very rapidly after being drawn from the cow, it is the practice of many good dairymen to raise the temperature of the milk to 100 degrees when set. In this way, they get a quicker and more complete separation of the cream as the milk cools down.

It would be a good idea to have, in all butter factories, apparatus for setting milk so constructed that the temperature of the mass of milk can be gradually and evenly raised to 100 degrees, or even slightly above; for it is difficult to deliver warm milk in a good condition—especially in hot weather if it has to be carried any considerable distance, while in cold weather, it is sure to get considerably reduced in temperature, both in milking and on the road to the factory. Hence, it seems almost absolutely essential, if the best results are to be attained, to have some means of properly raising the temperature of the milk at the factory.

COOLING AND AIRING.

If milk is to be sent to the factory, for either butter or cheese making, where the distance is half a mile or more, it should be aired and cooled—especially if it is to be shut up in a tight can. This cooling should be done as speedily as possible after milking, to avoid taint or souring. If the milk is kept over night, such airing and cooling are absolutely indispensable. The mode of doing this must vary with conditions and circumstances; but, whatever method may be adopted, we would by no means recommend putting ice directly into the milk. The effect cannot be to improve flavor or keeping quality.

PROTECTION FROM THE HOT SUN.

By no means should the can of milk be exposed to the direct rays of a hot sun, either on the platform waiting for the delivery wagon, or on the wagon. Give it shelter and shade of some kind, in both cases. If a woolen blanket is wet in cold water and wrapped around the can, the rapid evaporation from the blanket will keep down the temperature. Everything that can be should be done to preserve milk in its normal condition.

TREATMENT OF NIGHT'S AND MORNING'S MILK.

The night's milk and the morning's milk should never be mixed before starting for the factory, but kept in separate cans and so delivered. The effect of mixing will be seen soon enough at the factory, and often much too soon in hot weather. If the morning's milk were made as cool as the night's, the effect of mixing would not be so speedy and disastrous. But it appears to be an immutable law, that reducing the temperature and then raising it hastens decomposition. A low temperature only retards decomposition; it does not prevent it, unless very low and it is continued. As soon as the temperature is raised, decomposition sets in with accelerated rapidity, as if to make up for lost time. Hence, we have always looked upon low temperatures in the dairy as objectionable. As low as 60 degrees but not below 50 degrees is the limit which we prefer. We think this range more effective for long keeping than a lower one. Certainly, dairy goods made and kept within this range will not go to decay so soon as in a higher temperature.

RECEIVING.

In receiving either milk or cream from the patron, it is essential not only that justice be done in the weight or measure, but that the patron should be satisfied of this fact. The agent sent out to gather cream should be an honest man, in whom the patrons as well as the employer have confidence, and should understand his business and do it in a workman-like manner, so as to inspire confidence. He should also be versed in the various tricks that may be resorted to by patrons to deceive and cheat, and be on his guard, quick to discern any suspicious surroundings or indications. As much depends on his judgment and observation as on his honesty—especially if any of the patrons are disposed to be dishonest, as is sometimes the case where it would generally be least suspected. The later device of not only measuring cream by the gauge, **but of testing** its yield of butter by churning a sample, **is** not only a guard, to considerable extent, against fraud, **but more** closely approximates justice by getting **at** the **actual** quality of the cream, on which depends its value. There is no associated system yet devised—save that of churning every patron's cream separately and weighing the product—that **secures** exact justice to all. Nature does not appear to have furnished standards of commercial measure or value for the purpose of indicating mine and thine in mixed transactions, or in speculative exchange. We have only relative and approximate guides, by which justice, in a business sense, is by no means secured.

TESTING.

Where milk is delivered at the factory, we have as yet no **standard** test of value. All the receiver can do is to see that it is **in a** normal condition—neither sour nor tainted, nor containing bad odors. For this purpose, the smell must mainly be relied on. Hence, healthy and keen olfactories are a great aid here, as in some other cases. If one catches the fumes when the can cover is first removed, or as the milk runs into the weighing can, he is pretty sure to detect any very positive bad odor.

The eye, to one of experience, is almost certain to detect any great variation. Even slight watering is seen by some from the peculiarity of the reflection of light from the surface—especially when in motion. Much water shows from the "thin" appearance of the fluid. Where the smell or appearance are cause for suspicion, or there is any other cause, a sample may be saved and such tests as are at hand may be applied. The so-called lactometer will show whether the specific gravity is below or above the normal standard. The cream gauge will give the per cent. of cream at a given temperature. If, afterward, a sample right from the herd, taken so as to know that it has not been tampered with, shows better quality by these two tests, it is pretty conclusive evidence that the milk from which the factory sample was taken was not in a normal condition. If the herd has been subject to no change of feed or conditions between the times of taking the two samples, any jury would be safe in bringing in a verdict against the defendant for watering, skimming, or otherwise tampering with his milk, as the facts in evidence might indicate.

BAD MILK.

Sour or tainted milk, to any perceptible degree, ought not to be received at the factory. One such mess will injure, if it does not spoil, a whole batch. The sour milk is likely to lead to a sour, leaky batch, and the tainted milk to huffy if not floating curd, and porous, quickly off-flavor and decaying cheese. We have little patience with those who deliver such milk, and none with those who attempt to devise means to work it into palatable cheese and thus to get it into the unsuspecting stomachs of the consumers. It is too much like making omelets of rotten eggs. This is especially the case with tainted milk. The first stages of souring are not so objectionable, so far as wholesomeness is concerned. Sour milk may make good pot-cheese to which we do not object, but it will not make good American cheddar cheese. To attempt to work it into this is the worst use it can be put to.

WEIGHING.

All possible precautions should be taken to avoid mistakes in weighing and giving credit. A hasty comparison of each mess with that of the previous one delivered by the same man will indicate any marked departure from weight and serve as a check against error. It is well to always announce the weight to the patron, who then has a chance for comparison with his average or previous messes. He will be pretty likely to mention any marked variation, especially if it is against him. Some patrons like to have a pass-book, in which the weight of **each** mess is entered. This is a little trouble to the **receiver** when in a hurry, but it is a complete check against errors of entry on the factory book, and against the forgetfulness of the patron, who may get the impression that he has delivered more milk in a given time than he has been credited with. Everything that guards against error or misunderstanding will be found to pay and give satisfaction to honest men. An honest factoryman not only wants to be right, but to appear right and have the confidence of his patrons. A dishonest one will want to appear right, and it is well to take such precautions as will make him what he appears. See that the weighing can is properly balanced, that the scales are true, and that the weights are correct. An honest man will bear watching, and it is absolutely necessary to watch a rogue. Where the milk is sold to the factory, of course all interest in the matter with the patron ends when he gets his milk correctly weighed and his money for it. Where the *pro rata* system is carried out, this interest extends to the weighing of the cheese, its marketing and the division of the proceeds.

KEEPING MILK.

When the milk is in the cheese vat, it should be stirred and aired at night until the temperature is down to 70 degrees, if it is to stand quiet; if an agitator is used, which is preferable, no further attention need be paid to the milk but to see that the supply of cold water is ample and continuous. As to mixing the morning's with the night's milk, it appears to be preferable to working up the two milkings separately.

BUTTER MAKING.

THERE really are but four systems of setting milk for cream, notwithstanding the numerous inventions and devices. These are: 1. Cooling in water; 2. cooling in air; 3. shallow setting; 4. deep setting.

DEEP SETTING AND WATER COOLING.

Deep setting, whether in **pails** or pans, is **always** accompanied with water **and the use** of ice. In many instances, **however,** where running **w**ater is abundant, ice is dispensed **with,** and the pails are **set** in pools or tanks, while the pans have water run around them, if not under them. Under-cooling, however, is pretty well understood **to be a** disadvantage, unless the vessel containing the **milk is** submerged in water or nearly so. Ice is a good **deal used,** and the milk rapidly run down in temperature. Some think this is the better as well as the quicker way, if not the only way to get all the cream. Our only objection to this rapid cooling is that it runs the temperature too low, and, in our opinion, injures the keeping quality of the product.

EFFECT OF TOO LOW COOLING.

If run below 40 degrees, or the point where water begins to expand, all cooling below that point lessens the difference in specific gravity between the water and the fat globules, and operates diametrically in the opposite direction to what is desired. The aim is to condense the water, which is a good conductor, and leave the fat globules, which are poor conductors, unchanged or but slightly contracted. In this way, the heavier fluid settles and drives the light particles of fat upward to rest on the surface. But, if we go below 40 degrees, we produce the directly opposite effect and retard the rising of the cream. For quality, we prefer the slower cooling in water, and think the longer time given will secure all the cream available and in a purer condition.

BUTTERMILK FLAVOR.

If more cream or butter is obtained by rapid cooling, we think it is because more particles of caseine are entangled in the cream and remain in the butter when churned. This would of course make more weight for market, but of inferior quality and sooner to go off flavor. But where the butter is consumed fresh from the churn, this does not matter so much; and if the particles of caseine give the butter a slight buttermilk flavor, it pleases some palates that have been educated to like it. We, however, prefer the sweet, delicate flavor of cream butter, free from caseine or lactic acid. But, if one has a special line of customers, he must please them, whatever the demand may be. If the butter is thrown on the general market, and there is liable to be delay in getting it into consumption, it cannot be made too pure, nor retain its rosy flavor too long.

BUTTER MAKING.

SHALLOW SETTING AND AIR COOLING.

Generally, in shallow setting, whether in large or small pans, cooling the milk in air is depended upon. Formerly, an underground room, or one in a shady place, was the only appliance usually resorted to for cooling. But, of late years, some method of artificially cooling the air by the use of ice is generally adopted. In some cases, the milk room is made small, with low ceiling and double walls, so that a cake of ice near the ceiling does the cooling. Usually, however, some sort of refrigerator construction is resorted to, so that cool air from the ice-house, or ice placed above the milk room, is introduced to regulate the temperature and keep it steady. We prefer cooling in air, though it may take a little more space and time. By this method, extremely rapid cooling and low temperature are avoided, and no violence is done to the milk or cream. Deep setting, it is true, exposes less surface to the air; but if the milk is not submerged, the surface is likely to be cooler than the air above, and to condense the vapor in it, which falls with all its impurities on the surface of the cream. Any foulness or bad odors are thus absorbed and go into the butter product. While submerging obviates this objection and keeps out all impurities from the air, it also prevents all escape of bad odors by evaporation. Whatever that is objectionable may be in the milk is retained there. By setting in open air, which should of course always be pure and sweet, the air, being cooled down and used as a medium for cooling the milk, takes up the exhalations of moisture and odor from the milk, and thus purifies it. The colder medium is always the condenser and absorbent, and it is only when the milk gets colder than the air above it that it condenses the moisture in the air and absorbs its odor. This will never occur where cold air is the cooling medium. The milk theoretically can never get cooler than the air, while practically it remains a degree or two warmer than the air.

OXYDIZING CREAM.

There is another advantage in using the air as a cooling medium. In shallow setting, more surface is exposed and the air, coming in contact with the surface, imparts to it a portion of its oxygen, which mingles with the oils and develops that fine butter flavor so much relished by most and which is a peculiarity of fine butter. Again, slow cooling gives more time for this oxydation to go on, and thus " ripen " the cream for churning without souring it. This leaves all the fine flavor in it, unmixed with flavors resulting from acidification. But, where milk is set deep for creaming—and especially where there is no exposure to the air, as is the case in submerging—no butter flavor is developed, and the cream has to be kept until sour before it is properly oxydized. There is not a full development of butter flavor proper, but development of flavor resulting from the mingling of lactic acid with the oils. But without this exposure and acidification, the butter is insipid and comparatively flavorless. Any subsequent exposure to the air soon throws the butter off flavor, the oxygen mingling with the fats alone while the cream is rising and still sweet. This development of flavor by oxydation is not mere theory; it has been scientifically demonstrated at Cornell University, New York, if not elsewhere, and must sooner or later be generally accepted and butter making proceed on a more rational and certain basis. But it is hard work to get people out of old ruts, or to overcome fixed habits and prejudices. Really scientific butter making, in which every step will be thoroughly understood and deliberately taken, is a thing of the future. It will come in time, and then our descendants will wonder why we were so stupid and slow as not to see and adopt the simplest principles when they were thrust into our very faces. But mind and judgment are matters of growth, the same as everything else in this universe of being.

SKIMMING MILK.

So many improvements or inventions have been introduced in the setting of milk for cream that the term "skimming" has become almost a misnomer. In both deep and shallow setting, arrangements have been made in several of the patent pans and cans for drawing out the milk from the bottom and leaving the cream. Glass gauges are set in the vessels so that the exact depth of the cream can be seen, and the milk drawn down close to the cream or a small amount of the upper portion of the milk left with the cream. In skimming with a skimmer or dipper, many aim to take the upper portion of the milk, on the theory that the separation is less perfect toward the top than it is lower down. Especially may this be done where a dipper or skimmer without holes is used. It is claimed by some careful experimenters and close observers that this adds to the quantity of butter yielded without deteriorating the quality.

WHEN TO SKIM.

Whether skimming off the cream or drawing off the milk be practiced, the question arises as to the proper time for performing the operation. The more general practice is to "skim" just as the milk gives unmistakable signs of acidity, or thickens a very little on the bottom of the pan or can. A few prefer to skim the cream sweet, and still another few let the milk lopper. This wide divergence of opinion and practice shows how very imperfectly is the real philosophy of butter making understood; but, notwithstanding this, each one is usually very tenacious in his belief as to the superiority of his own practice. A few fancy butter makers say that the finest butter is made from sweet cream, raised in cold air by shallow setting. It is insisted by them that airing and oxydizing, and not souring, is what "ripens" cream and fits it for easy churning, while this airing and oxydizing imparts the fine aroma so much desired in the finest butter. This view of the origin or development of flavor is sustained by experiments made at Cornell University, at the suggestion or under the supervision of Prof. L. B. Arnold. It is also claimed that the lack of flavor and the short-keeping of sweet-cream butter churned from cream raised by deep setting is due to its lack of oxygen, and that souring the cream thus raised, before churning, both oxydizes it and imparts a ranker and more positive flavor resulting from the effects of the lactic acid. We think both propositions look reasonable, and we should like to see a series of scientific experiments made to determine both the effects of oxygen and the effects of lactic acid on the butter product of cream. At present, theory and practice vary so widely with different butter makers who turn out a high-priced butter for the market, that one is led to doubt all theories and query whether the quality of butter does not depend on something not yet known, which is independent of all current theories and practices.

CHURNING.

And as to the proper time of churning, there is an equal divergence of opinion and practice. One churns his cream sweet, another wants it slightly changed, a third wants positive acidity in the cream, and a fourth loppers the cream, while a fifth lets the cream stand even twelve hours after loppering—and this extremely sour cream butter sells for the very highest market price. So we are left all at sea, so far as acidity is an element in butter making. Again, to further illustrate these extremes, while a gentleman in Vermont is setting his neighbors agog by raising cream in a vacuum, a Canada gentleman is experimenting with an invention to raise cream by hydrostatic pressure and get the fat of the milk so pure as to dispense with churning. We hope both will succeed.

TEMPERATURES.

There is not so wide a difference in opinion and practice as regards the temperature at which churning should be done in order to secure the best results; yet there is quite a wide range—from 55 degrees to 65 degrees—or 10 degrees Fahrenheit. But only a few go as high as 65 degrees or as low as 55 degrees. The great majority favor 60 degrees to 63 degrees as the proper range of temperature for different seasons and conditions. Some favor 58 degrees to 69 degrees, and all appear satisfied with results. It is not improbable that different degrees of acidity in the cream require different degrees of temperature for churning, and that sweet cream requires still another variation of temperature. So the breed, condition of the cows, kind of feed, quality of feed, character of the water drank, length of time the cows have been in milk, and other considerations, require variations in the temperature. Sure we are that the difference in conditions and surroundings must explain some of the differences of opinions and practices among butter makers.

WHAT MAKES THE BUTTER COME.

It is not known whether concussion or friction, or both, cause the separation of the butter from the buttermilk in churning. But we suspect that concussion is the real agent that produces the separation, as we have really seen no churn that did not in some **way** produce more or less concussion. All the **churns** we have seen used appeared to produce good results, **and** we find every dairyman is satisfied with the work of the churn he uses, whatever the kind, style or patent. We cannot, therefore, recommend any style of churn as superior to another, but we prefer the simple and less expensive

BUTTER MAKING.

forms, as not only costing less but being easier to keep clean.

The churning should be steady and not violent. A too **rapid or** sudden separation of the butter from the buttermilk is not desirable. It is no recommend for a churn that it churns quick. Such a churn is apt to injure the so-called grain of the butter and make it salvy and greasy. The least churning that will separate the butter from the buttermilk is the best.

WHEN TO STOP CHURNING.

The improved modern method, **now** in practice by **the** best butter makers generally, is to stop the churn **as** soon as the butter is collected in particles the size **of** wheat kernels. Just before this, when the first signs of the separation of the butter is seen, the sides of the churn are washed down with cold water—usually below 60 degrees, or about 55 degrees—to not only prevent waste, but to harden the butter and make it easier to handle. When the granules are the size of wheat kernels, the **butter is drawn** off or the butter taken out of the buttermilk, as the case may be. If the butter is left in the churn, water is poured in to float the butter, which is then gently agitated a moment and the water drawn off. This operation is repeated until the water runs clear. Sometimes one of the washings is in brine, which coagulates the caseine into a soluble form and prepares it to be washed out afterward. In this way, it is believed that purer, longer-keeping butter can be made. In some cases, however, butter makers have customers who want a buttermilk flavor in their butter They, therefore, do not wash the butter, or wash it very little. Such butter must be consumed at once, as it will not keep.

WORKING.

By this method of retaining the butter in a granulated form, only sufficient working is required to evenly work in the salt. The less working the better.

SALTING.

The salt, after the butter is properly drained, can be carefully mixed with the butter by stirring. When thoroughly incorporated, barely pressing the butter together into a solid mass is all that is needed. If one does not want butter very salty to the taste, it can be evenly and nicely salted by completely wetting it with saturated brine, then carefully pressing the granulated butter together and leaving in it as much of the strong brine as will remain. We have seen butter salted in this way, and it was very evenly and completely salted, having in it no undissolved grains of salt, but it was not as salt to the taste as some like.

About an ounce to the pound is good salting; but more or less salt must be used to suit the taste of customers. None but refined salt should be put into butter. No salt is better for this purpose than the Onondaga F. F., which is American, and the cheapest salt fit for dairy use that can be obtained.

The principal office of the salt in butter is to impart an agreeable flavor, in conjunction with the natural aroma of fine butter; but it is a fact that too much salt

BUTTER MAKING. 77

injures good flavor, and it may, to some extent, be used to cover up or neutralize bad flavors. We do not recommend its use for this latter purpose, preferring that the natural flavor of butter from pure cream should be preserved.

SALT AS A PRESERVATIVE.

Salt does very little to preserve butter. It retards the decomposition of the caseous and albuminous materials left in it; but if butter is properly made of cream not mixed with loppered milk and is completely washed with pure water, it is a fair question if butter will not keep longer without salt than with it. There are instances on record where butter has been kept sweet without salt for a long time. We half suspect that, though salt at first retards decomposition, the salt itself, in time, decomposes and becomes sodium and chlorine gas, or enters into new combinations with the constituents of the butter, and thus makes new compounds that do not in the least improve the flavor. We have no positive evidence of this, but have had this suspicion awakened by facts related about the keeping of butter and by a process of general reasoning. It is true that salt is one of the most stable compounds known, but we have proof that it can be resolved into its original elements, when stronger affinities are presented for one or both of them to unite with. It would not, therefore, be strange if such decomposition sometimes follows when used in our food preparations.

PACKING BUTTER.

It is quite a knack to properly pack butter in large packages, and the work needs to be carefully done. Some use it too violently, by pounding it down, and thus making the butter greasy or oily. It should be gently pressed together in the package in such a way as to leave no spaces filled with air, for the air will surely mingle with the surrounding butter and injure its flavor. A good way is to begin the pressure at the center and work carefully toward the circumference, so that all air may escape at the sides. In this way, perfect solidity of the mass is secured, and it is left in the best condition for keeping, so far as the packing is concerned.

PREPARING THE PACKAGE.

Before putting the butter in the package, the package should be soaked in water, so as to remove the taste of the wood, and then thoroughly soaked in saturated brine, so that the wood will not draw the salt from the butter which comes in contact with it. If it does, the butter thus deprived of salt will turn white, have a sickish flavor, and soon turn rancid. It is a good idea to not only sprinkle a thin layer of salt over the bottom of the package, but to rub the moist inner sides with dairy salt, and thus make sure that there is salt enough in contact with the wood to prevent its absorbing the salt from the butter.

CLOSING THE PACKAGE.

When a package is filled, a piece of thin muslin, cut so as to just fit into the top of the package and completely cover the butter, should be wet in cold water and carefully placed over the top, having the edges pressed down close to the sides of the tub. Then the cloth should be completely covered with a thin layer of salt;

and if the salt is moistened, so as to form of it a thick paste that will become air-tight when it dries, it will do much to keep the top of the butter clean and sweet—for the more nearly air tight the package is when completed the better it is for the preservation of the butter. Then put on the cover, and seal the whole as tightly as possible.

STORING.

Remove the package to a cool, sweet place, not above the temperature of 60 degrees, and set it so that it will absorb no moisture or odors from the ground. Much butter is spoiled by keeping, because of neglecting the temperature, and setting the bottom of the package directly on the cellar bottom. If kept at a temperature above 60 degrees, butter will surely go off flavor, and wood will as surely draw moisture from the ground, if in contact with it, and become sour and musty, sooner or later affecting the flavor of the butter within the package. Nothing is to be lost, but all to be gained, by paying attention to these little things.

STYLE OF PACKAGE.

Of course, **where** a maker has a special market for his butter, he will put it up in such style and form of package as suits his customers. He needs no other guide and would injure his business if he followed one. But, for general market purposes, the 50 lb. tub is the best form. The New York and Boston dealers like this because it is convenient for the retailer, who can readily slip the tub off from the butter for either weighing or cutting up for his customers. But aside from these considerations, the Welsh tub is a very bad form of package for keeping butter, as it is by no means air-tight nor anything approaching it. Hence, butter sent to market in these tubs must soon be sold and go into consumption, or there is material depreciation in quality and a corresponding loss in price. The old-fashioned firkin, which could be headed up and the butter covered with brine, is a much better package for keeping butter. But, where butter is consumed as fast as it is made, and fresh winter made butter supplies the demand through the cold season, the keeping of butter for any considerable length of time is not of so much consideration. We think it fortunate that this is so.

CHEESE MAKING.

SO much has been written and said, and so little understood, about cheese making, that it seems almost a hopeless task, as well as a thankless one, to attempt to say anything more on the subject. Sour ignoramuses and floating charlatans have spoiled more curds than have been spoiled by any defect in the milk. Sour, whey-soaked cheese has been the rage, and it is generally supposed that acid alone makes a firm cheese, when the experience of every cheese maker is that it is very difficult, by the ordinary processes, to make a firm curd out of sour milk—which, of course, no one ought to be asked to make into cheese—unless it be pot-cheese. Acid may make a curd solid, but not until it has cut out a large share of the goodness of the curd, and the cheese resulting will be about as digestible as so much putty.

DUTY OF PATRONS.

It is the duty of every patron of a cheese factory to send good milk to it, and to send the milk in good condition. It is not only his duty, but his interest to do this. A bad mess of milk may spoil a whole vat-full. This not only entails loss on his neighbor, where the factory is run on the *pro rata* plan, but the patron must stand his share of the loss. Aside from the loss entailed on **others** and himself, he ought to be ashamed to deliver milk **in a** bad condition. There is no valid excuse for **it.** It ought to be his pride to deliver milk in as good condition as anybody does. If he cannot, he should leave the business, and go into something in which he has the ability to excel. Care and cleanliness, if the cows are healthy and have proper food, will insure good milk always.

UNREASONABLE EXPECTATION.

It is unreasonable to expect a cheese maker to turn a prime article of cheese out of poor milk. If one carries shoddy cloth to the tailor, he expects a shoddy suit in return, not a broadcloth one. So, if he carries bad milk to the factory, he must expect bad cheese. If he takes sour apples to the cider mill, he does not expect sweet-flavored cider, but sour. So, if he carries sour milk to the cheese factory, he must **expect sour cheese.** These defects, when they exist in a small **degree,** may **be** overcome, or nearly so, and a passable cheese made. But, is the cheese made from imperfect milk really a fit article of food? Who would work rotten eggs into custard, or sour meal into bread? Yet this is just as consistent as working sour or tainted milk into cheese, and **t**he product is just as wholesome. That which **mak**es stinking eggs makes stinking milk—decayed albumen—which is just as wholesome in the one as in **the other.**

GUARANTEES.

The cheese maker who guarantees his cheese is very foolish if he does not insist on a guarantee of good milk, nor should he be compelled to rely on his judgment formed in the haste of receiving the milk. A tricky man may juggle a bad mess of milk on to the best expert. How can the cheese maker tell whether the milk is from a gargetty udder, or the first milk after calving—both **of** which may develop in a very offensive way when the milk is heated up? So the milk may be so nearly tainted or so nearly sour that it will not stand the process of heating up and cooking. The law ought to be very severe on the man who delivers bad milk at a factory, or sells it to anyone. The factoryman who pays the price **of** good milk for sour or tainted milk is certainly very short-sighted, and cannot long maintain the respect of the man who sells it to him, nor sustain himself pecuniarily. The man who pays cash for milk has the right, above all others, to demand that the milk shall be sweet and wholesome. This is one point that should be insisted upon—the delivery of good milk in good condition.

HEATING.

After the milk is all in, or the requisite amount is in the vat, the heat may at once be started and raised to some point between 80 and 86 degrees. If we set below this, the rennet works too slow; if we set above, it is thought to work too fast—so custom has fixed upon this range of temperature for setting, and there appears to be no valid objection to it. But while the temperature of the milk is being raised, and before, it should receive frequent stirrings to keep the cream from rising, and thus becoming partially or wholly wasted. The rennet should by no means be added until the temperature stops rising—or so nearly so that by the time the rennet is stirred in and the stirring stopped, because the milk begins to coagulate, **a** stationary temperature will **have** been reached.

COLORING.

The coloring fluid should be added just before **the** rennet is—unless white cheese is made. There is a limited demand for white cheese for the London market But do not make the color **too** high—as there is a limited demand for high-colored goods, **and** this mainly **from** the South, in spring and fall. Nor should the color be too pale, as there is really no demand for **pale** cheese. It should be either white or of a medium hue—a bright, golden yellow. There is a demand for uniformity **of** color, as buyers often **want large** lots, all of the same hue **or shade.** In **selecting such a** lot, they may **rule out** first-class cheese **that is** to pale **or** too high-colored. The universal use **of the same** manufacture of coloring extract guaranteed of uniform strength, might secure uniformity in coloring. But this is doubtful and difficult. A better, and we think, a feasible way, would be to have a standard color—like those accompanying paints—furnished to every cheese maker **as** a guide, and let him color to it **as** nearly as possible. In this way, **a close** approximate to uniformity of color might be secured. He could then use whatever coloring fluid he chose, and his eye would **be his guide.** Coloring does not improve the product. **If it does no** harm, it does no good beyond gratifying the eye and deceiving the palate through the common notion that high color and high flavor go together.

SETTING.

Theoretically, 98 degrees or blood heat would seem to be the temperature for setting, as rennet is the most active at this point. Usually, 82 degrees in warm weather, and 86 degrees in cool weather, are the points at which the rennet is added in setting. But there is no reason for a different temperature at different seasons, except that in cool weather the temperature is liable to run down a little—which should not and would not be the case, if the make room were so constructed that the temperature could be controled and kept at summer heat.

OTHER DETAILS.

Enough rennet should be added, as a rule, to cause thickening of the milk to begin in 20 minutes, at 82 degrees. More or less rennet may be used, as it is designed to have cheese cure more or less rapidly. As a rule, the more rennet is used, the lower should be the temperature at which the milk is set and the curd worked. Agitation of the milk should be kept up for at least 15 minutes, where coagulation begins in 20 minutes, or as long as it can be and not prevent a solid coagulation. The stirring after the rennet is incorporated is merely to keep the cream from rising. The less cream gets to the surface, the less waste there will be. In a cool room, where the surface cools quickly and there is a falling of the temperature of the milk, there will be a thin cream on the surface. This will form a soft cream curd, which will adhere to the sides of the vat, to the rake, and to the hands, and be quite annoying. The amount is trifling, but the annoyance of the thing is enough of itself to make it desirable to keep the cream down; and a summer temperature of the room is useful for this purpose, aside from the comfort and the better handling of the curd, from first to last.

KEEP THE TEMPERATURE EVEN.

After the milk begins to thicken, a cloth should be thrown over the vat to keep the surface warm. A convenient way is to tack a cloth to slats a little longer than the vat is wide, putting the slats a foot or eighteen inches apart. This is easily rolled up and set aide, when not wanted, and is easily unrolled over the vat when needed. There should be no raising of the temperature after the rennet is added and the mass comes to a standstill. If there is, the portion next to the sides and in the bottom of the vat will get the most heat, and there the rennet will work the fastest and the curd will become tough before it is firm enough on the surface. Therefore, let the heat be stationary after the rennet is added and until the curd is cut fine, and keep the heat as even as possible all this time.

CUTTING.

The coagulum should be cut as soon as it will break clean across the finger when placed in it and lifted gently upward. This early cutting is essential. There is seldom, if ever, any waste from cutting a curd too soon. The clearest whey will always be obtained by cutting early. The whey exudes from the curd much more freely when it is yet young and tender—and the only object in cutting the curd at all is to get out the whey. When cutting is begun, let it be continued as expeditiously as possible until it is finished. Do not stop and let the curd stand and toughen. It cuts more easily, with less friction and less waste by loosening fine particles of curd, when it is tender and parts easily before the knife. The more it toughens, the harder it cuts, the more friction there is, the more the curd is torn and bruised, and the more the waste. If we could cut **early and** cut instantaneously, it would be all the better.

CUT FINE.

Cut the curd very fine. **Seldom**, if ever, is a curd cut too fine. As the object **is to** get rid of the whey, the finer it is cut, the more easily we achieve our object. It is not as far from the center of a small piece of curd for the whey to run out as it is from the center of a large piece. By cutting fine, we expose more surface for the whey to run out of, and we have smaller pieces to heat up. Curd is a bad conductor of heat. If the pieces are large, it takes a long time for the heat to slowly penetrate them when we want to increase it. The small pieces, therefore, absorb the heat more evenly, and this gives an evener action of the rennet.

"COOKING."

After the cutting is done, if the whey is separating rapidly, the heat may be started at once. If the action of the rennet is rather slow, it is better to **wait a few minutes for the curd to harden a little, while with your hand you carefully rub down the side of the vat, thus removing all the** curd that may be adhering **to it.** Not over five **minutes** waiting, as a usual thing, is necessary, **and** generally there need be no waiting. But as **soon as the heat is** started, begin to gently stir the curd **with a rake, by** passing it down into the middle of the **vat and** gently raising the curd on each side. If uncut pieces appear, carefully separate them with the teeth of **the** rake. Keep **up** this stirring, which may be more violent after the curd hardens, until **the whole is** heated **up to** 98 or 100 degrees—or to **blood heat. The** reason **for** constant agitation is to keep **an even** temperature throughout **the mass** and prevent the **curd from packing.** This secures even **action** of the rennet. **The reason for** going to blood heat **is** because rennet is **most active at** this point. **It is the temperature** indicated by **Nature.** It is **the one at which we digest our** food, and the **one** at which the **calf's stomach forms curd** and afterwards digests it. **The** pepsin or **gastric** juice is more potent at blood heat, **and** this pepsin or rennet is what does the work. The heat does not cook the curd in the vat any more than it cooks the milk in the cow's **udder. We** choose 98 degrees as the proper temperature **because the** digestive or cheesing process of **the rennet goes on faster** at this point. To go above or below it is **to lose instead of gain.** This temperature should **therefore be maintained until the** curd is "cooked" —that is, **until the action of the rennet has expelled the proper amount of** whey and the curd is as firm as we want it. Anent the stirring of curds, use the hands as little as possible. There is nothing better for this purpose than the common hay rake with the handle shortened and one tooth cut off from each end by severing the rake-head within three quarters of an inch of the next tooth·

DRAWING THE WHEY.

We next draw the whey down to the curd—leaving enough to stir it in easily, and cool the whole mass down to 90 degrees, to avoid too much packing, and draw off the balance of the whey. The whey should be run off before the acid develops, because acid, formed from the milk in the sugar, dissolves the minerals and cuts some of the oils in the curd, and these run off in the whey. Many curds, by remaining in the whey too long, become whey-soaked, and make cheese that is soggy and hard, with a sour flavor. This kind of firmness is not desirable, notwithstanding it is called for by buyers, who seldom know anything about cheese making. If the acid develops before the whey is properly expelled, or the curd fs "cooked," it carries off the minerals, which are in the form of phosphates, and this makes the cheese poor indeed. These phosphates are of lime, iron, magnesium, etc., but the principal is phosphate of lime. The affinity of these minerals for lactic acid is stronger than for phosphoric acid; so they let go of the latter and unite with the lactic acid, forming lactates and leaving the phosphoric acid free. But if we get all of the whey out of the curd that we desire, and then get the curd out of the whey—that is, draw off the whey—before the acid comes on, we retain the phosphates and fats in the cheese—all the goodness that belongs in it. The acid will come on afterward, but we have reduced the sugar to a minimum, and the amount of acid developed does no serious injury. As the whey is already expelled, of course it cannot wash out the minerals that are dissolved. These remain, and in the process of curing recombine with the phosphoric acid. We have left in the curd about $3\frac{1}{2}$ parts of the 87 parts in 100 parts of milk. The whey left in the curd contains, we will say, 1-10th of the sugar that was in the milk. The acid formed from this, though too small to do any known injury, is large enough to do all the good required, if it does any good at all. We are, therefore, safe when we get the whey out of the curd and the curd out of the whey before the development of the lactic acid.

SALTING.

When the whey is well out of the curd, so as not to waste the salt, the salt may be applied and stirred in. The salt does not stop the development of acid, as is popularly supposed. When applied, it aids in keeping the curd loose. Then the curd may stand, with occasional stirring, almost any length of time for the purpose of airing and cooling, of getting rid of any bad odors, of developing flavor by oxydation from contact with the atmosphere, and of letting the acid come on. It is safest not to put the curd to press until it has a positively clean sour smell. This shows that certain chemical changes have taken place, freeing the curd of the gases generated by this process, and prevents any huffing of the cheese on the shelf in the curing room. Where cheddaring and grinding are practiced, the salt is of course applied after the curd is ground. Cheddaring is the easier and safer method, as the whey can be drawn early, and there is no danger from the acid. Salting at the rate of $2\frac{1}{2}$ lbs. of salt to 1,000 lbs. of milk is the usual practice and not far from right. For long keeping, 3 lbs. of salt are not too much. Use none but the best dairy salt—the best of all the dairy salts, as well as the cheapest, being the Onondaga, F. F.

PUTTING TO PRESS.

After the acid fermentation is properly progressed, the curd should be put to press at a temperature not much below 80 degrees, nor much above 85. If higher, it is liable to heat and taint the cheese at the center; if lower it is difficult to face the cheese and press the curd together properly. But in warm weather, there is not much danger of getting the curd too cool.

ACID IN CHEESE MAKING.

THIS has been written on so much that the subject has become hackneyed. The acid seems to have eaten into the souls of some and turned them sour; but notwithstanding, the so-called "sweet curd" idea has made steady progress. Much of the opposition has come from buyers for export, who do not appear to be able to distinguish between a firm cheese and a hard cheese, and who ignore quality if they get a cheese hard enough to ship, without danger of breaking, by the time it is ten days old. This has been demonstrated by the fact that cheese condemned when green as too soft has been pronounced by the same buyers fine and all right, even endorsed with enthusiasm, when it was two or three months old, which is about as young as a first-class cheese should be shipped.

ANALYSIS OF MILK.

Of course, there would be no acid in milk if there were no sugar in it. The proportion of sugar is shown by the following analysis of an average sample of good milk made by Dr. Voelcker, the late chemist of the Royal Agricultural Society of Great Britain:

ACID IN CHEESE MAKING.

```
Water..................................................87.30
Butter.................................................3.75
Caseine...............................................3.31
Milk-sugar and extractive matter............4.86
Mineral matter (ash)..........................0.78
                                              ──────
          Total................................100.00
```

It will be seen by this that the per cent. of sugar is at least 4.50, if we deduct the extractive matter, the proportion of which is not given. Numerous German analyses show it to range from 3.50 to 5.75 per cent. Henry and Chevalier put the average at 4.77, and Prof. L. B. Arnold says milk from cows in perfect health should contain, during the month of August, 4.30 to 5.50 per cent. We will call it 4.50 per cent. There is 87.30 per cent of water.

WHAT THE CHEESE MAKER DOES.

In separating the solids from the liquids, by the action of rennet, at the proper temperature, we expel, say 83.30 parts of the water, leaving 4 parts. We get rid of, say 4.20 parts of the sugar, which is held in perfect solution in the water. We lose, say .50 of one part of butter, .31 of one part of the caseine or albuminoids, and .13 of one part of ash. This leaves—

```
Water ..................................................4.00
Butter..................................................3.25
Caseine...............................................3.00
Sugar...................................................30
Ash......................................................65
                                              ──────
          Total................................11.20
```

We thus have 11.20 per cent. of the 100 parts out of which to get our cured cheese. A fair average is 10 lbs. of cheese for 100 pounds of milk. Some of the water evaporates in curing, say 1 part, leaving 3 parts. Our 10.20 parts of cheese is then composed of the following:

```
Water................................... .3.00
Butter.................................. .3.25
Caseine ................................ .3.00
Sugar, or what results from decomposition.. .30
Ash .................................... .65

        Total..................... 10.20
```

This is a little in excess of the general yield. The waste is usually in the greater amount of ash, sometimes nearly the whole of it, when the acid develops before the whey is expelled. In that case, the lactic acid dissolves the phosphates and they run out with the whey. This is so much loss of ingredients absolutely essential to digestion and assimilation.

WHAT OUGHT TO BE.

So far from this, there ought to be less loss of ingredients than we have supposed in our illustrative figures. But more of the butter is cut and runs off with the whey when the acid is developed before drawing the whey. The aim of the "sweet curd" system is to avoid this waste as much as possible, especially that of the butter and ash. To effect this, the whey is drawn sweet and the acid allowed to develop after the curd is cooked and the whey expelled. There need be no more water left in the curd, but more butter and ash, both of which tend to make the cheese softer. But with proper curing rooms, there is no trouble in making the cheese firm enough for all practical purposes, including shipping. It is better to use less rennet and not have coagulation begin under 25 minutes, cutting the curd about 15 or 20 minutes later, and

ACID IN CHEESE MAKING. 95

to take more time for curing, at a lower temperature. We then have a firmer, more buttery, and better flavored cheese, which is a desideratum. But, with high and changing temperature in the curing room, no certain or satisfactory results can be counted on.

THEORY AND PRACTICE.

In theory, **we ought** to prevent the waste of **butter** and caseous matter altogether; but in practice, there is always a little loss of butter, and there are certain albuminous ingredients, called by the Germans *ziega*, which rennet will not coagulate. There is, of course, no means of saving this. The sugar we cannot and do not want to **save** in the cheese. If retained, it would be injurious and probably spoil the **cheese,** as the lactic acid in the small amount of sugar **retained in** the water is all that we can well manage. But all matter coagulable by rennet, all the butter, **and** all **the** ash, we ought to retain; **and** we cannot really call ourselves scientific cheese **makers** until we can do this. When accomplished, **a great**er weight of cheese will be the result.

There is no avoiding the acid resulting from the small amount of sugar retained in the curd; but, having expelled sufficient **whey,** if we keep the curd warm enough, and hold it in the **vat or** the sink long enough, the lactic acid will come on and we shall get rid of the bad results of putting a curd to press sweet. This acidity is absolutely necessary **with** the generality of curing rooms. But with low and steady temperature in the curing room, we can do about as we please.

RENNET.

OUR recent observations more than ever convince us of the importance of good rennet in cheese making. Great evils and losses result from the use of bad rennet; and the great trouble is that many cheese makers do not know when rennet is bad. There is not only the evil of diseased and tainted rennets, to begin with, but the preparation from good rennets is often spoiled in the preparing. Frequently, in hot weather, they are allowed to taint while soaking; and when the liquid is prepared sweet, it is often allowed to ferment and taint for want of sufficient salt and from exposure in a high temperature.

SOAKING IN WHEY

Soaking in whey, containing all its taints and impurities, is the source of a vast amount of foul rennet and off-flavored cheese. If whey is used, it should be boiled to kill taints and precipitate, as far as possible, the solids remaining in it. But, do the best that can be done with it, and still whey is objectionable for soaking rennets, because of the acid that develops in it from the presence of sugar. This acid neutralizes a corresponding amount of rennet and helps to impoverish the cheese. Indeed,

RENNET. 97

if carried far enough before the curd is removed from it, the finer flavoring oils are cut by it, the phosphates are dissolved, and these pass out with the whey, leaving the cheese but little better than an indigestible mass. If the acid adds solidity to the cheese, it does it by removing from it valuable ingredients.

TAINTED RENNET.

Frequently, we have encountered rennet preparations that were not only very sour, but also tainted and having a strong smell of carrion. Nothing but huffy, porous, stinking and rotten cheese can result from the use of such rennet preparation. Yet it is used, and the result is attributed to bad milk, or to the presence of some inscrutable taint or ferment, so prone are mankind to attribute effects to wrong causes. It has been to us unaccountable that cheese makers should use such horrid broth as we have seen them use, if they have any sense of smell whatever, and utterly astonishing that they should expect good cheese to be made from using it. With good milk, the cheese may appear fairly good for several days—especially if put to curing at a low temperature. But sooner or later, the taint must make its appearance. Possibly, it may not show ten days from the hoops, but the cheese can never become a mellow mass without also becoming a stinking one. It will soon be ripe and soon rotten.

CURING RENNETS.

It is usually understood that rennets are calves' stomachs salted and dried, or otherwise prepared; but it is not so certain that all the rennets in market are of this kind. The stomachs of the young of all milk-eating animals may be used for curding milk. We are not so sure but that among " Bavarian " rennets we get the stomachs of the young of every animal known under the sun. They are of all sizes and all degrees of strength, but are generally liked by those who use them. They are cured by tying the two ends, and blowing the rennets up, like bladders. A better way, we think, is to rub them well with pure dairy salt, stretch them on a hoop or crotched stick, and hang them in a cool dry place. Some simply fill them with salt, tie them, and hang them up to dry. A great objection to this is, that the salt is likely to draw moisture from the atmosphere, and in wet weather the rennets are liable to drip and thus lose strength. Salting rennets down in a barrel, as we do meat, is considered objectionable—for what reason, we know not. The writer had excellent "luck," one season, with rennets preserved in this way. In whatever way preserved, rennets should, by all means, be kept cool. Heat is found to be very injurious, while cold—even freezing and thawing—appears advantageous. Possibly because the freezing and thawing loosen the fiber and set the rennet spores free.

AGE AN ADVANTAGE.

No rennets less than a year old should be used, if it can possibly be avoided. The old rennets, other things being equal, are stronger and make a firmer curd than new ones. Any one who has experimented with both will

RENNET. 99

always aim to have a supply of good old rennets on hand.

SAVING RENNETS.

In saving rennets, great care should be **taken to have** them right. The fourth stomach of the **calf is what is** saved. Cut it from the adjoining stomach, at the point of junction, and **do not** leave a piece of intestine on the other end, but **cut** close **to** the opening of the rennet. Remove straws and dirt of all kinds carefully, but be sure to not **rub** off the delicate lining of **the** stomach, which is **the** digestive or coagulative part **and very much** inclined **to** adhere to your hands, especially **if they are dry**. Do not try to rinse off **anything more** than the loose dirt, and that without **rubbing,** for you cannot rub without waste. What is **better,** avoid having dirt or any thing else in the stomach **to** remove. This you can do by letting the calf go sixteen or eighteen hours without eating, and placed where it can get hold of nothing to swallow before killing. Say, feed it at night and slay it the next day about noon. The stomach will **then be** empty **and** clean and well stored with pepsin **for the digestion of** the next meal. This secretion is just what you want. The rennet is **best** when the calf is six or eight days old. But, in any **case,** digestion should be well established before killing. **If the** calf should go too long without food—as is often the case with veal calves—the stomach will get inflamed. This is objectionable

SELECTING RENNETS.

In selecting rennets to soak, all discolored and bad smelling ones should be scrupulously rejected. But rubbing rennets is a disagreeable and disgusting business, and it is somewhat difficult to keep your rennet of uniform strength. Therefore, if good rennet extract can be bought at a reasonable price, we would recommend its use. It ought to be made better and cheaper in a wholesale way than in little batches at each factory. To guard against imposition, one should buy only of known reputable dealers. Preparing your own rennet is much like doing your own shoe making. It doesn't pay, if you have got anything else remunerative to do.

WHOLESALE PREPARATION.

If one must prepare his own rennet, the better way is to do it in a lump before the cheese-making season begins. Get a strong barrel and a pounder—such as used by washerwomen; also a wringer. Take old rennets and cut them into strips. Make a weak brine of pure water, by using one pound of salt to twenty pounds of water, and in this, soak, pound and wring your rennets. Hang them up and freeze them; then soak, pound and wring them again; and so on as long as you can get any strength. When done, carefully settle, skim and strain your liquid. Put it in a clean barrel or stone jars, put in all the salt that it will dissolve, so that a little will settle on the bottom, then stop or cover tight; put in a cool place and take from it as wanted for use. There is nothing better than saturated brine for keeping animal products. Be sure, however, that you use only the purest dairy salt in preparing brine. Some say that only stone jars should be used for keeping rennet. We have used

RENNET.

an ash tub for the amount prepared weekly. To keep the wood from tainting, we invariably, every time we dipped out rennet and exposed new surface, rubbed it with salt.

EXCLUDING AIR.

Rennet could be much more easily kept sweet if put in an air-tight vessel. The "American Dispensatory" says: "When gastric juice is completely protected from the air it may be kept unchanged for a long time; but on exposure it speedily undergoes decomposition, acquires a very offensive odor, and loses its characteristic digestive property." We think that the Dispensatory is right. The composition of pure gastric juice is as follows: Water, 97.00; salts, 1.75; pepsin, 1.25; total, 100.00. There is also a small amount of free acid. Both rennet extract and pepsin are used as medicine.

CURING ROOMS.

IT is hard to determine which is of the greater importance, good **rennet** or **properly constructed curing-rooms**; for both are necessary **to the production of** the best cheese, while the want **of either is sure to injure** if not to spoil it. The importance of **controling the temperature** in curing has not yet taken hold **of the popular mind.** The best milk in the world may be spoiled **by** bad rennet, and the best curd in the world may be spoiled by **a** bad curing-room.

TEMPERATURE.

In a large majority of the curing-rooms of the country, the temperature ranges from 60 degrees Fahrenheit to 90 degrees and even above. Sometimes these extremes are realized within a few days. Think of setting a curd to fermenting at 80 to 90 degrees, when it ought **to start at** 60 to 65 degrees! Yet, this is frequently **done; and to** prevent the cheese from huffing and crawling **it is proposed** by some to make the curd **so dry and sour in the** beginning that heat will not soften **it. In this way, is** made what some buyers style a "firm" **cheese. The best** English cheddars, according to the **American Encyclope-**

RENNET.

dia, are set to curing at a temperature of 60 degrees, and are never allowed to go above 70 degrees. Our observation and experience are that the range of temperature should never go above 75 degrees. Curing should begin as low as 65 degrees, and no cheese should be marketed under thirty days from the hoops. When the curing is slow, as it ought to be, the cheese will not be ripe in less than that time. If sixty days old before ready for market, the better. The hurrying process is everywhere bad for the product, and no amount of souring helps the matter, however hard it may make the cheese and however well it may stand up in hot weather. We want something else besides standing-up quality. With a low and even temperature for curing, we do not need to work all the goodness out of the curd to make a firm cheese. We do not have to cut the fats and phosphates out with acid, nor to dry all the moisture out by fine cutting and high scalding or long scalding. We can stop the cooking when the curd is evenly cooked through so as to be springy when pressed together by the hands, take it out of the whey before the acid develops, and put it to press without unnecessary delay.

AN EXAMPLE.

In the fall of 1884, we ate some cheese at Mr. N. L. Brown's, Gurnee, Ill., which was dipped sweeter and put to press softer than we ever thought of doing; yet the cheese was close-grained and fine-flavored, and one that would pass muster as a first-class cheese anywhere. But it was not cured in a hot curing room, nor in one where the temperature went up and down the same as it did on the outside of the building. It was placed in his cellar, at a temperature of 64 degrees, and there remained until it was fit to cut. Nor was it even rubbed, but occasionally turned over. When cut, it looked like a cheese that had been kept in a box a year, covered with mold and mites. The superfluous moisture was dried out but the butter was all left. It demonstrated what can be done by temperature. Had this cheese been cured in an ordinary curing-room, it would have gone all out of shape in a few days—as soon as rapid fermentation set in—and been off flavor by the time it was ten days old. Several other cheeses were cured in the same cellar, in the same way, but none of them were put to press so soft or sweet, but all sweet-curd cheeses, and all buttery and fine. This particular one was the result of hurry, as other matters than the curd demanded attention. But the thought came that it would be a good experiment, as it was, and the result was satisfactory, though not different from what was expected. Cheeses made in the same way as the others that were cured in the cellar, and some cooked more and soured more, were made by the same gentleman and cured in an ordinary curing-room. In hot weather, they swelled and some of them got out of shape, while the flavor was sharp and rough. But those in the cellar, at 64 degrees, apparently never moved a hair's breadth out of shape, were as solid as old butter, yet firm enough for shipping even, and of the finest flavor. It is hardly necessary to say that the cellar was exceedingly clean and sweet, and was well ventilated. These cheeses were a demonstration, if not a revelation.

MOISTURE IN CURING.

It should be remarked, by the way, that a curing-room does not want to be a dry room. We do not want to dry cheese; we want to cure it; that is, let it go through the proper chemical change. This it does best in a somewhat moist room, in which the surface does not dry and become hard and impervious, so that the gases cannot escape. It is better to contend with a little mold than a dry atmosphere.

BETTER CHEESE CAN BE MADE.

We see, on turning to Prof. Arnold's "American Dairying," that he says: "The temperature of a curing-room for whole milk should be 65 to 70 degrees; for part skims, 75 to 80 degrees." It is thus seen that fat plays an important part in curing. "The more fat," he says, "the cooler may be the room; and the less fat, the warmer may it be." Again: "Under the present state of things, a cheese that will stand a voyage of 4,000 miles can hardly be called a fancy cheese. * * * But a much fancier cheese than we are now producing, one that will stand shipping, can be made. To do this will require milk to be free from some of the imperfections which are now quite common; it must be transported to the factories in much better ventilated cans; *it must be made with less rennet and less acidity; and it must be cured in an even and lower temperature.*" We mark the conclusion in *italics*, because we believe these are vital points. We insist that we cannot do ourselves credit nor realize the best financial results in cheese making until we build better curing rooms rooms in which we can control the temperature without fail. We have not yet settled down to cheese making. We are still trying experiments and resorting to temporary expedients. We must build far more deliberately and for permanency. It is not necessary that we should point out just how a building may be erected so as to give control of the inside temperature. Architects know how to do it. When our cheese makers get to the point where they demand such buildings, they will get them without much trouble and at moderate expense. It is only necessary that they should have the "will." The "way" will speedily open.

WHEY.

WE notice that, in some localities, the patrons of the cheese factory are very much interested in the question of the value of whey for feeding purposes— some going so far as to assert that what is left of milk in cheese making is as valuable as what is removed! This is a startling assertion, and, if true, would convict our dairymen of a vast amount of stupid waste. Is it true? Let us try to get at the facts of the case by a direct, common-sense investigation of it.

COMPOSITION OF MILK.

We will begin with the composition of milk. From hundreds of German analyses, ranging from 81.30 to 91.50 parts of water, we take a fair average analysis, which we think will do justice to the mixed milk of our best cheese factories:

Water............87.18	Sugar............	4.21
Caseine............ 4.21	Ash...............	.60
Albumen .... .55		
Fat 3.24	Total..........	99.99

WHAT IS TAKEN OUT BY CHEESE MAKING.

Now, in making cheese, what follows? We ought to secure all the caseine, but we do not quite. There is a small waste. We loose all, or nearly all, of the albumen. We leave in the whey most of the sugar, if we do not convert it into acid before getting rid of the whey, in which case we may have an injurious amount of the acid in the curd, besides dissolving and washing out nearly all the ash, which is composed of phosphates, principally of iron, magnesia and lime. These are changed into lactates, leaving the phosphoric acid free—not a very good food for anything but rats. We ought to save nearly or quite all the ash—the phosphates. But by the ordinary process of cheese making, these are nearly all lost, as is shown by the analyses of whey, which probably accounts for the low estimate in the popular mind of the value of cheese as food, it being rated at one-half the value that it would have were the phosphates all retained. But, four-fifths of the nitrogenous and muscle-making material has been removed, and also nine-tenths of the fat, which is heat producing and some say furnishes motor power. We have retained in the cheese 5.84 of the 12.82 parts of solids, leaving 5.98 parts, 4.21 parts of which are sugar and not wanted in the cheese, or, at most, only a fraction of it. We leave less than one part of the albuminous and caseous matter, which is the most valuable, and only one-third of one part of fat. So there is less than one part of solids left besides sugar, and the rest of the whey is water.

COMPOSITION OF WHEY.

What is whey, then, but sweetened water, using sugar of a very low sweetening quality, with a fraction of albu-

WHEY.

minous matter and ash in it? Again, by the so-called "sweet" process, which retains all, or nearly all, the phosphates in the cheese, the whey is made still poorer by analysis. Only the sugar and a fraction of the albuminous matter, not coagulated by rennet, is left in the whey; and the amount of sugar in milk varies considerably, ranging, in a large number of German analyses, from 3.0 to 5.48 per cent. of sugar. But let us more closely examine the composition of whey. An average of eighteen analyses made by Voelcker is as follows:

Water	.93.02	Sugar	} 4.99
Nitrogenous matter	.96	Lactic acid	
Fat	.33		
Ash	.70	Total	100.00

POOR STUFF.

Thus it is very plainly to be seen that whey is poor stuff to feed, even in its best estate. It has some value to mix with other foods, if used sweet; but when the sugar has all turned to acid, and the phosphates have become lactates, leaving the phosphoric acid free, the whey is abominable, and can be used only in small quantities and with great care. It ought not to be fed to young animals with tender stomachs, and does older animals no good.

CRUELTY TO ANIMALS.

All this corresponds with general observation and experience. The most intelligent dairymen with whom we are acquainted do not consider sour whey worth drawing home. It is cruel to feed sweet whey to any animal exclusively. Even a hog, which has made its growth—and no animal can more fully extract the nutrihealth while actually growing fat on sweet whey. The portion of less than one per cent. of albuminous matter prolongs, rather than sustains life. That is to say, the hog will not starve to death quite so quick if fed whey as it will without it. The sugar accumulates in the system as fat, while the hog is slowly perishing of inanition. But if it is thus cruel to feed it alone to full grown animals, it is doubly so to feed it to young and growing animals—as pigs and calves—the necessities of the lives of which demand tissue-making material as well as life-sustaining. If whey is used, let it be fed sweet, and always with some **kind of dry** nitrogenous food, as bean meal, oil meal, pea meal, clover, etc But, with the acid system of cheese-making, it is impossible to do this. The whey is decomposed before run into the whey-vat.

THE END

CONTENTS.

PREFACE... 3— 4

HISTORICAL—In Asia; Among the Jews; In Southern Europe; In America; Figures from the Census; Growth in Thirty Years; Product per Cow and per Capita; Home Consumption vs. Exports; Forms of Milk Consumption; The Private Dairy vs. the Factory...................... 5— 12

CONDITIONS—Pastures; Water; Winter Food; The Stable; Shelter; The Dairy House; Cleanliness; The Herd. 13— 17

DAIRY STOCK—Points of a Milker; Dutch-Friesian; The Jersey; The Guernsey; The Ayrshire; The Shorthorn; The Devon; The American Holderness; Inbreeding; Swiss; Polled; Hereford; Common Stock................ 18— 34

BREEDING DAIRY STOCK—Selection; Coupling; Care.. 35— 39

FEEDING STOCK—Carbonaceous and Nitrogenous Foods; What is Carbon? What is Nitrogen? Compounding Rations; Per day and per 1,000 lbs. Live Weight; Sample Rations; Fattening Rations; Working Rations; Digestibility of Foods; Elements of Foods; Ensilage; Remarks... 40— 52

HANDLING MILK—Keep Quiet; Regularity; Keep Down the Foul Odors; Keep Out the Dirt; Let Out the Cows; A Lick of Meal; Care of Milk; Composition of Milk; Deterioration of Milk in the Udder; Do Fats Expand Before Congealing? Effects of Falling Temperature; Cooling and Airing; Protection from the Hot Sun; Treatment of Night's and Morning's Milk; Receiving; Testing; Bad Milk; Weighing; Keeping Milk............... 53— 66

BUTTER MAKING—Deep Setting and Water Cooling; Effect of Too Low Cooling; Buttermilk Flavor; Shallow Setting and Air Cooling; Oxydizing Cream; Skimming Milk, When to Skim; Churning; Temperatures; What Makes the Butter Come; When to Stop Churning, Working; Salting; Salt as a Preservative; Packing Butter; Preparing the Package; Closing the Package; Storing; Style of Package. .... 67— 80

CHEESE MAKING—Duty of Patrons; Unreasonable Expectation; Guarantees; Heating; Coloring; Setting; Other Details; Keep the Temperature Even; Cutting; Cut Fine; "Cooking;" Drawing the Whey; Salting; Putting to Press.. 81 - 91

ACID IN CHEESE MAKING—Analysis of Milk; What the Cheese Maker Does; What Ought to Be; Theory and Practice... 92 - 95

RENNET—Soaking in Whey; Tainted Rennet; Curing Rennets; Age an Advantage; Saving Rennets; Selecting Rennets; Wholesale Preparation; Excluding Air   96 - 101

CURING ROOMS—Temperature; An Example; Moisture in Curing; Better Cheese Can Be Made.................102 - 106

WHEY—Composition of Milk; Composition of Whey; Poor Stuff; Cruelty to Animals..............................107 - 110

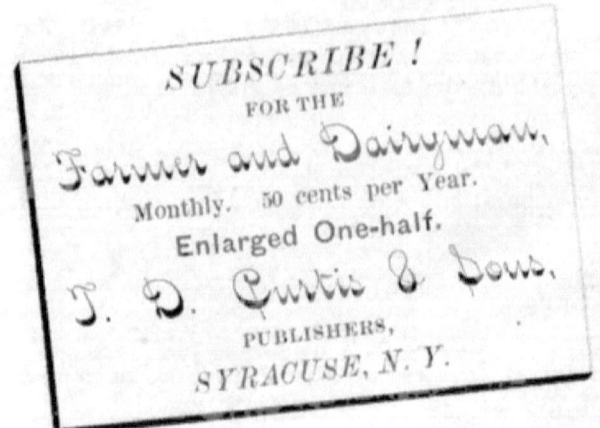

SUBSCRIBE!
FOR THE
Farmer and Dairyman,
Monthly. 50 cents per Year.
Enlarged One-half.
J. D. Curtis & Sons,
PUBLISHERS,
SYRACUSE, N. Y.

www.ingramcontent.com/pod-product-compliance
Lightning Source LLC
Chambersburg PA
CBHW022141160426
43197CB00009B/1379